The Meaning and Philosop

THE IBIS WESTERN MYSTERY TRADITION SERIES

The heritage of all Western spirituality, both open and esoteric, and all the systems, theories, and practices that relate to it, are drawn from a single source: the Judeao-Christian spiritual tradition. This tradition has yet deeper roots in the distinctive religious faiths of the great civilzations of Egypt, Greece, and Mesopotamia.

At the heart of all these great traditions lies their ultimate goal: the spiritual regeneration of humanity. There is more than one Way to its attainment, and it is the totality of the many paths that lead us back to our primal source that constitutes the Western Mystery Tradition. They are encapsulated in the countless texts that enshrine and reflect the work of the inspired men and women who have dedicated their lives to preserving, interpreting, and transmitting this tradition.

Many of these text have become a part of the canon of Western literature, but there are many others that have been unjustly neglected, hidden in times of persecution, or have simply gone unrecognized. Some record exalted inner experiences, some are guides to esoteric practice, while others are speculative studies of esoteric knowledge and spiritual wisdom. All of them have one feature in common: an inherent power to enrich us spiritually.

It is from rare printed versions of these unknown or forgotten texts, and from studies of them, that the Ibis series of classics of the Western Mystery Tradition is drawn.

—The Editors at Ibis Press

See page 157 for a list of
titles in the series

The Meaning
and
Philosophy
of
Numbers

Leonard Bosman

Foreword by R. A. Gilbert

Ibis Press
An Imprint of Nicolas-Hays, Inc.
Berwick, Maine

Published in 2005 by
Ibis Press, an imprint of
Nicolas-Hays, Inc.
P. O. Box 1126
Berwick, ME 03901-1126
www.nicolashays.com

Distributed to the trade by
Red Wheel/Weiser, LLC
P. O. Box 612
York Beach, ME 03910-0612
www.redwheelweiser.com

Library of Congress Cataloging-in-Publication Data

Bosman, Leonard.
  The meaning and philosophy of numbers / Leonard Bosman ; preface by Robert A. Gilbert.
      p. cm. -- (The Ibis western mystery tradition series)
  Originally published: London : Rider & Co., 1932.
  ISBN 0-89254-138-5 (alk. paper)
    1. Symbolism of numbers. I. Title. II. Series.
  BF1623.P9B56 2005
  133.3'35--dc22
                                                    2004056852
VG
Cover design by Kathryn Sky-Peck
Printed in the United States of America
10   09   08   07   06   05
6   5   4   3   2   1

CONTENTS

FOREWORD vii

INTRODUCTION 11

    I.   CREATION BY NUMBER 33

    II.   THE PREPARATION OF
           THE COSMIC FIELD 50

    III.   THE ABSOLUTE, THE NO-NUMBER OR
           CIRCLE POTENTIAL 66

    IV.   THE NUMBER ONE 70

    V.   THE NUMBER TWO, THE DUAD 78

    VI.   THE NUMBER THREE 87

    VII. THE NUMBER FOUR 96

    VIII. THE NUMBER FIVE 107

    IX.   THE NUMBER SIX 116

    X.   THE NUMBER SEVEN 125

    XI.   THE NUMBER EIGHT 138

    XII. THE NUMBER NINE 143

    XIII. THE NUMBER TEN 148

FOREWORD

In the course of a lecture on "The Theosophic Doctrine of the Zohar," Gershom Scholem, the greatest kabbalistic scholar of the 20th century, distinguished between the classical and contemporary senses of the term "theosophy." The latter, he wrote, was "a label for a modern pseudo-religion."[1] Such a distinction is not unusual among academics, who tend to look askance at the Theosophical Society, but Scholem added a footnote in which he argued that, ". . . the famous stanzas of the mysterious *Book [of] Dzyan* on which Madame Blavatsky's magnum opus, *The Secret Doctrine* is based owe something, both in title and content, to the pompous pages of the Zoharic writing called *Sifra Di-Tseniutha*.[2]

Scholem went on to support his argument, but admitted that he was not the first to suggest this. That honor went to "L. A. Bosman, a Jewish Theosophist, in his booklet *The Mysteries of the Qabalah* (1916)."[3] What he did not state was that Bosman fitted the definition of a theosophist in both senses: not only was he an active member of the Theosophical Society, but he was also concerned with perceiving and describing "the mysterious workings of the Divinity."

Leonard Bosman was born on November 2, 1879, at Stepney in east London, into a Dutch Jewish family that had settled in England some 20 years earlier. Almost nothing else is known of his private life, save that he was later married, to Sarah Mills, and that he had three daughters. He seems to have spent all of his life in London, but his education, occupation, and even his date of death remain in obscurity. His work, however, should not.

Bosman remained true to his Jewish faith throughout his life,[4] and studied under a gifted but little-known kabbalistic teacher, Elias Gewurz, with whom he would co-operate in publishing a remarkable series of "Esoteric Studies." But Bosman was never confined by Judaism; he also sought for spiritual experience and expressions of spiritual reality in other creeds. As a young man he joined the Theosophical Society in order to further this quest, and absorbed its ethos of tolerance toward all religions. His search also led him to Freemasonry, but as a theosophist—and perhaps as an expression of his emphasis on social and religious tolerance—he chose to enter Co-Masonry, the form of Freemasonry that admits both men and women as members, rather than the masonically regular United Grand Lodge of England.

Neither the precise date of his initiation, nor the Lodge in which he was made a mason are known, but it probably took place around 1910, for by 1919 he was both a Past Master of his Lodge—a process that would have taken seven years or more—and a Past First Principal of his Royal Arch Chapter.[5] Despite his deep involvement in Co-Masonry, Bosman was still able, in the years around the beginning of WWI, to contribute a number of mildly controversial articles on philosophical and spiritual aspects of Masonry to *The Freemason*, the most influential masonic publication of its time and a pillar of masonic regularity.

At the same time, he was a regular contributor to *The Co-Mason* and, after a split within the Co-Masonic ranks in 1925, to its rival, *Freemasonry Universal*. This would seem to be an unusual progression, for Bosman was an independent thinker and yet he followed the Besant-Leadbeater branch of both the Theosophical Society and Co-Masonry: organizations predicated on unwavering obedience to the Masters and to their earthly representatives. Whatever his reasons for such ill-advised loyalty, Bosman was clearly content with the Adyar version of theosophy. Throughout the 1920s and 1930s he wrote regularly for *The Adyar Bulletin* and for *World Theosophy*, his highly speculative contributions reflecting his preoccupations with morality, human freedom, spirituality, and metaphysics.

If this had been his only contribution to human knowledge it would have been respectable but virtually unknown. Bosman's real claim to being a gifted and significant speculative writer lies with his published books. And these, though little known and often little in size, are many in number. Between 1913 (*Towards the Summit*) and 1932 (*Sleep on it. A Key to the Nature of Dreams*), he published fifteen books under his own name, five with Elias Gewurz and one with Anita Orchard. Of these, two are masonic, three concern theosophy, seven are kabbalistic, and nine cover what might be termed "speculative philosophy." The most substantial and the most important is the present work, *The Meaning and Philosophy of Numbers*.

It is essentially a kabbalistic study, which is only fitting for it was with the Kabbalah that Bosman began his esoteric career. But before considering this, other aspects of his work should be assessed. Bosman's masonic works are original and interesting—Philip Wellby, a confirmed Grand Lodge mason, commended *Studies in Freemasonry* (1931) for "the sincerity, power, and beauty of [the author's] exposition of the symbolism of the Royal Arch degree," and noted that, "He has succeeded in transmitting to the reader some part of that Light of Masonic Wisdom of which he himself is happily possessed."[6] His theosophical studies are more varied. Both *Studies in the Secret Doctrine* (1915) and the earlier *Teachings of Theosophy Scientifically Proved* (1914), which was edited by Elias Gewurz, are unexceptionable, but *H.P.*

Blavatsky: The Light-Bringer (1932), his joint work with Anita Orchard, is a less happy effort.

This was criticized, justifiably, by Frank Lind as "a panegyric from start to finish" that "sounds too good to be true."[7] He further noted that the authors' uncritical adulation led them to make contradictory statements. And yet Bosman had been astute enough to see the connection between the *Sepher Dzeniutha* and the putative "Stanzas of Dzyan" and to point it out in his first kabbalistic study, *The Mysteries of the Qabalah* (1913). This book was the first of five in the series of "Esoteric Studies," issued between 1913 and 1917 under the guidance and with the aid of Bosman's teacher, Elias Gewurz. A later edition of *The Mysteries of the Qabalah*, published in Chicago in 1922, provides a subtitle, "written down by seven pupils of Elias Gewurz and prepared for publication by one of them," that indicates the existence of an otherwise unrecorded private and speculative kabbalistic school in Edwardian London.

The five "Esoteric Studies"—the others are *The Cosmic Wisdom*; *The Music of the Spheres* (in two parts); and *The Sacred Names of God*— were the first fruits of this school, but while they contain much fascinating speculation and not a little sound information, they do not represent Bosman's mature thought. For that we must turn to *The Meaning and Philosophy of Numbers*.

The kabbalistic essence of the book is clear from the outset. Bosman states that numbers are primarily "symbols of the beginning and development of the universe" (p 12) and builds upon this foundation. He considers the interrelationship of "figures, numbers, music, and cosmic progression" and their nature as expressions of God, but he has no interest in the vulgar, predictive art of numerology. His prime concern is rather with "the true Inner Reality behind Number, that Reality, the Rhythm of the Universe, which reflects itself unerringly in the science of Mathematics" (p. 30). All of this he might well have drawn from purely kabbalistic sources, but Bosman draws upon a broad and eclectic range of authorities: on academic philologists, Pythagoras, Cornelius Agrippa, Gerald Massey, and on theosophists from H. P. Blavatsky to J. M. Pryse and G. A. Gaskell (neither of whom he names!).

In his analyses of individual numbers there are also clear parallels with the "Address on Numbers" delivered to Zelatores of the *Societas Rosicruciana in Anglia*. This address is restricted to members of the Society and Bosman is unlikely to have seen it, but many of the members were also active in the Theosophical Society and it is highly probable that the essence of its contents became known to him through discussions at Theosophical Society meetings. That he would have been in sympathy with such Western esoteric ideas (which are largely kabbalistic) is clear, for his book is concerned with the spiritual aspects of number and he presents these in a thoroughly Western manner.

Bosman also specifically eschews what he terms "the 'magical' side of the subject" (p. 30), for which he was commended by Ethel Archer in her review of the book: "the writer wisely touches on the definite dangers that may accrue to the unperfected man from studying the lore of numbers, since he is liable to make first hand acquaintance with the great powers behind them."[8] It is possible that his caution owes something to a knowledge of Algernon Blackwood's novel, *The Human Chord*, which takes as its theme the terrible risks that such studies may incur. And yet it is surprising that, for all his immersion in kabbalistic studies and Freemasonry, and his sympathy with Western Hemeticism, Bosman was never involved with any esoteric order. Perhaps his commitment to the Theosophical Society ran too deep to permit a rejection of Eastern approaches to esotericism, but his absence from Western hermetic circles is almost certainly the principal reason for his work being largely unknown or ignored.

He deserves better, for what he writes has a value of its own. It is not derivative, but original. As with all authors of integrity, he draws upon his predecessors, not simply to repeat what they say, but to build upon their work and to create his own vision of spiritual reality: a reality to be accessed through symbols, of which numbers are among the most potent. Numbers are also significant in Freemasonry, as Bosman knew well. He was active in what are known as the "additional degrees," and current ignorance of the man and his work can be likened to the fate of the Corner Stone in the Mark Degree. It is initially "heaved over" among the rubbish and lost from sight. But the culmination of the degree involves its recovery and restoration to a place of honor. It would be no more than is due to him if the work of Leonard Bosman were to be similarly recovered and restored to the light.

R. A. Gilbert
Bristol, England
May 2005

NOTES

1. Gershom Scholem, *Major Trends in Jewish Mysticism* (New York: Schocken, 1946), p. 206.
2. *Ibid.*, note 2, p. 398.
3. *Loc. cit.* Scholem was wrong about the date; *Mysteries of the Qabalah* appeared in 1913.
4. In 1926, his book *A Plea for Judaism* was published in India by The Association of Hebrew Theosophists.
5. The Holy Royal Arch of Jerusalem is a distinct masonic degree but is considered to be also the completion of the Third Degree. Bosman was a member of Star in the East Chapter of the Royal Arch, and probably of Hermes Lodge, which met at the same address in Lauderdale Road, in west London.
6. Review of *Studies in Freemasonry*, in *Occult Review*, vol. LV, no. 1 (1932):59.
7. Review of *H. P. Blavatsky: The Light-Bringer*, in *Occult Review*, vol. LV, no, 3 (1932):207.
8. *Occult Review*, vol. LV, no. 5 (1932):349.

INTRODUCTION

It will probably be conceded that despite the many books on the subject of numbers there is much mystery attached to their inner meaning. Almost all of these innumerable publications appear to have copied from one another and may all be traced back to a common origin in the mind of Pythagoras himself. Though he did not put his teachings into writing, yet several of his followers and later writers attempted the task with more or less success.

The writers of these modern works on numbers, though they have much to say on the magical property of such ideas as may be contained in them, seldom seem to concern themselves with the fundamental meaning behind all numbers, nor do they explain why they attach to them the different meanings accepted blindly by the devotees of the science. Hence it is hoped that in this work a little of the true nature of numbers may be unveiled so that it may be shown not only what they represent in fact, but also what they are in idea.

At the outset of such a study, however, the first consideration should be an understanding of the words and terms used in connection with the science of numerology. For, although words and terms in themselves necessarily imply limitation, they are, nevertheless, the sole clue to the ideas originally underlying them. To this end an ordinary acceptation of the meaning of terms will not carry the

student very far. Reference after reference to the
ordinary dictionary will leave him all too conscious
of the impossibility of understanding by such means
the depth of meaning and the true idea behind the
term.

It is the involution of language rather than its
evolution with which reckoning has to be made. The
original meaning of a word in the language of its
birth is first to be traced to the very sound of the
letters which form its root. Unless this can be done
many difficulties will arise, for such roots in the course
of time have been blended with others and have
inevitably been misapplied by those who have
not known their original meaning. In this way
words have come to be applied to objects and ideas
which originally they did not represent. Thus the
true meaning has become, as it were, fossilized,
embedded in layer after layer of dissimilar meanings,
so that a thousand years later the birth of the
original root-sound and the meaning it was intended
to convey are all but undiscoverable.

This applies to the roots, but with the words
themselves there is even less chance of unveiling the
ancient meaning, so great are the changes brought
about by pronunciation, dialect, time and environ-
ment, and especially by the development of the
written word.

Primarily considered, numbers are symbols of
the beginning and development of the universe, of
a solar system, or a series of such, or, indeed, of any
rhythmic movement. The terms with which we
have to deal in considering the science of numbers
are figures, symbols, ciphers, arithmetic, and
mathematics.

The terms "numbers" and "figures" are usually considered as synonymous, but a little thought will show that this is not a true view. Thus, the figure 3 is not, strictly speaking, three, nor is it what is termed a number. It is merely a figure or symbol called by the name *three*, having a numerical value which is triune and representing that which will later be described as the threeing process of the universe.

A figure is, literally, something made, a shape or form (Latin = *figura*, a thing made). This shape or form acts in the case of the figures 1, 2, 3, etc., as a symbol (Greek *sym*, together; *ballein*, to throw), something thrown together, or put together, to form a sign or picture of an idea. Hence a figure cannot strictly be called a number, though it may represent it as a symbol.

What, then, is a number? Skeat states that the Indo-Germanic root of the word is *nem*. This is similar to the Sanskrit *nam* or *nama*, the origin of the word *name*. To name a thing is to individualize it or distinguish it (N) from the mass (M), and it is difficult to understand the difference between name and number, since the roots are practically the same. There is, however, a difference, which can be ascertained by a study of the roots of the two words.

Nem, the root of the word *number*, is probably Egyptian, although it may well be only naturalized in Egypt, being even older than the Egyptian language, which itself was derived from an earlier tongue. The Greek form is *nemo*, to distribute. Letter by letter *nem* explains itself : N represents an emanation or distinguishment, E a rhythmic progression from the mass, M. In this case the M symbolizes the completeness of the whole, that which includes all difference, all numbers, within Itself, which is not *one* in the sense of the beginning of all numbers, but that unification, or wholeness, which includes all numbers in itself as in solution, that from which all numbers spring in rhythmic progression.

If, however, as seems probable to the writer, the root is *num* rather than *nem*, the meaning is still clearer, for the letter U is the sound-symbol of that which links and makes possible a change of condition, and is so used in the Hebrew as well as in other languages. Hence *num* represents a coming forth, an emanation (N) from one state to another, (U) proceeding from universality (M) to differentiation.

The term *name*, on the other hand, is derived from the Sanskrit *nama*, a word formed, as far as can be seen, from two roots, *na* and *ma*, the former meaning *to individualize, to make distinct*, and the latter *to measure*. This dual root shows the real meaning most fully, for a name is thus that which distinguishes a person or thing and measures it, i.e. describes its kind or quality, its essential nature.

Thus figures, by their shape, represent the original ideas which they were intended to show forth. The names given to these figures, or symbols, should, then, by their sound, convey the same idea as does the figure by its shape. Hence numbers are names given to figures and represent the measures, or rhythms, or rhythmic unfoldment of all things under the generic title of numbers.

The meaning of the words used to name figures, *one*, *two*, *three*, etc., is not known in modern language. In Hebrew the words used to name or distinguish numbers can more easily be traced to their roots, thus making possible an understanding of their fundamental meaning and showing exactly why they were so named. Thus the word *one* does not merely mean a single thing, nor does the word *two* mean two things.

The word *one*, used to name the figure 1, is derived from the root sound *un*, as may be seen in such languages as Latin, French, German, and English. In Sanskrit and other tongues, however, the root is given as *ek* (*eka*, *yek*, etc.), and a similar sound, expressing the same idea, is heard in the Hebrew word *echod*, or *achod*. A comparison of these roots will clearly demonstrate the different conceptions of unity as understood by the ancients who named their numbers in this way.

The generally used European root *un* shows the idea of the passing from one state to another, from that which is symbolized and represented in the sound of the letter U, to the individualizing process as heard in the sound of forthcoming, the letter N. This gives the conception of a distinct and separate being (*en*, *ens*, being or a being), and shows that in the mind of the originator of this word there was the idea of a distinct and active individual power, which was therefore named *un*.

Whereas the European *un*, or *one*, represents number going forth to produce numbers, the Sanskrit, Hebrew, and Japanese words for *one* convey a conception somewhat different; *eka, achad*, and *ichi* (Japanese) all show the idea of division arrested, or numbers held in check, according, that is, to the sound–values of their roots, every letter having a deep meaning.

In the Cosmic Process of becoming, which number primarily represents, there is the Unconditioned All. This is not a manifested "number"—not, that is, a distinct and individualized number, neither one nor many, but simply the whole. Co-equal with the All is a certain potential power, symbolized by a point, and this point is seen symbolically as a *one*, as creation commences. The Point Unmanifest becomes the Power of manifestation, symbolized as a single definite stroke and called by the name One, meaning that which goes forth to produce change.

Thus the 1 is in the All, the 0 or Circle Potential, and acts with it to produce the Universe. The one in the nought polarizes it, as the human cell is polarized, and thus arise all numbers, the simple numbers, 1—9, emanating from the 1 in the 0 through this polarization. Hence in the beginning, the 1 and the 0 are *potentially* 10, i.e. complete and perfect, but have to become unfolded, as symbolized by the figures 1—10, before the Perfection innate within them can be manifested. This will be explained in the chapters which follow.

As is well known, the Hebrews, unlike the moderns, had no figures to represent what are called numbers, the letters of the Hebrew alphabet being themselves used to act as figures. The first ten letters, *Aleph* to *Yod*, A to I, are used to represent the figures 1 to 10 ; beyond this number other letters are added to these ten letters to form the higher numbers up to 19 ; then a change occurs, and the later letters are used to form the multiple numbers, the letter K standing for 20, the L for 30, the M for 40, and so on, the higher values being expressed by the final letters.

The Hebrews had also various mystic methods of understanding the sacred scriptures by a system of translating letters into numbers. Ascertaining the total value as numbers of any given word or words, they translated this numerical total into words once more, and showed deeper meanings in the original words than were at first apparent. As every letter had a numerical value, they were able to compare the numerical value of one word with another, and when two words had the same numerical value there was considered to be a deep connection between them. This method obviously lends itself to charlatanry and superficial thought, yet so much may be discovered by the use of it that it is not well to declare, as some writers have done, that the whole system is nonsensical.

The Greeks had a similar system, called by some "the Greek Kabalah", a system of numerology by means of which they endeavoured to understand Bible and other mysteries. Thus the famous number of the "Beast" of Revelations refers neither to Anti-Christ, nor even to the Kaiser, but when the letters which are the equivalents of the numbers are set down, the meaning is made clear. *Ho phren*, in Greek, is exactly 666, as is explained by the erudite author of *The Apocalypse Unsealed*, and refers to the earthly mind of man—mind drawn down into the vortex of passion and desire—a truly "beastly" mind, far less pure than the simple animal nature. Hence the "Beast", whose number, 666, is the same as that of a man, is nothing but the "beast" in man, the lower mind which, left to "gang its ain gait", will degrade man even beneath the level of the beasts.

B

"The fundamental geometrical figure of the Kabalah," says Madame Blavatsky (*The Secret Doctrine*, vol. iii, section x), "as given in the *Book of Numbers* (no longer extant), that figure which tradition and the Esoteric Doctrines tell us was given by the Deity Itself to Moses on Mount Sinai, contains the key to the universal problem in its grandiose, because simple, combinations. . . . The Devanagari (Sanskrit) characters . . . have all that the Hermetic, Chaldæan, and Hebrew alphabets have, and in addition the occult significance of the 'eternal sound' and the meaning given to every letter in its relation to spiritual as well as terrestrial things. As there are only twenty-two letters in the Hebrew alphabet and ten fundamental numbers, whilst in the Devanagari there are thirty-five consonants and sixteen vowels, making altogether fifty-one simple letters, with numberless combinations in addition, the margin for speculation and knowledge is in proportion considerably wider. Every letter has its equivalent in other languages and its equivalent in a figure or figures of the calculation table. It has also numerous other significations, which depend on the special idiosyncrasies and characteristics of the person, object, or subject to be studied. As the Hindus claim to have received these characters from Sarasvati, the inventress of Sanskrit, the language of the gods or devas (in their exoteric pantheon), so most of the ancients claimed the same privilege for the origin of their letters and tongue. The Kabalah calls the Hebrew alphabet the 'letters of the angels', which were communicated to the Patriarchs just as the Devanagari was to the Rishis by the Devas [*Gods or Powers*]."

The Chaldæans found their letters traced in the sky by the 'yet unsettled stars and comets' . . . while the Phoenicians had a sacred alphabet formed by the twistings of the sacred serpents." This is also found in the hieroglyphics and secret sacerdotal speech of Egypt, as the same writer remarks.

"The power and potency of numbers and characters", she continues, "are well known to many Western occultists as being compounded from all these systems, but are still unknown to Hindu students (with some exceptions), if not to their occultists. In their turn, European Kabalists are generally ignorant of the alphabetical secrets of Indian Esotericism. At the same time, the general reader in the West knows nothing of either : least of all how deep are the traces left by the Esoteric numeral systems of the world in the Christian Churches.

"Nevertheless, this system of numerals solves the problem of cosmogony for whomsoever studies it, while the system of geometrical figures represents the numbers objectively. . . .

"All beings, from the first divine emanation, or 'God manifested', down to the lowest atomic existence, 'have their particular number which distinguishes them and becomes the source of their attributes and qualities as of their destiny'. Chance, as taught by Cornelius Agrippa, is, in reality, only an unknown progression, and time but a succession of numbers. Hence, futurity being a compound of chance and time, these are made to serve occult calculations in order to find the result of an event, or the future of one's destiny. Said Pythagoras :

" 'There is a mysterious connection between the gods and numbers on which the science of arithmancy is based. The soul is a world that is self-moving : the soul contains in itself and is the quaternary, the tetraktys, the perfect cube.' "

It is to be noted here that Pythagoras is not reported as saying that the gods are numbers, or that all things are numbers, as some of his followers and critics affirm.

Many writers quote the Pythagoreans as stating that the whole universe and all things within it are founded on Number. Others say that Nature is ruled by a Law, of which Number is the form and measure, and that Number is manifested in all celestial movements. This idea is correct in the deepest sense, yet it has at times "caused the enemy to blaspheme". Most people understand numbers merely as figures, and know only that they may be used arithmetically, and therefore the idea that the universe *is built on Number* is, to them, simply nonsense, especially when, as is so often the case, such statements are made without explanation. Chaignet quotes Philolaus as saying that Number manifests its active presence in the movements of celestial and divine bodies, in the being of man, in his life, and all that which is thereby produced, in the Arts, and, above all, in Music. Apparently he does not see that it is not Number which is in all things, but that which Number represents. Apart from this, his work, *Pythagore et la Philosophie Pythagorienne*, is one of the best on the subject.

The rhythmic progression of the universe and of all creation is not, then, *caused* by numbers, nor is the universe, as some writers state, built on numbers.

Moreover, numbers are not to be found everywhere in Nature, as some enthusiasts declare.

Cosmic activity, staticity and dynamicity, action and reaction, movement and resistance, are the basic principles on which all Natural order is founded. The evolution and growth of a universe or of man, an idea crystallizing into form—all these have their stages of progression, definite transitions from state to state, the rhythms of the universe. These rhythmic progressions are so exact and so certain in their action that, transformed into earthly reckonings, they produce the only exact science, that of Mathematics, which is exact inasmuch as it is founded on cosmic verities.

Some writers consider that the Pythagoreans, being unable to explain the growth of a system in words, had recourse to numbers, as symbols of their ideas. This is, of course, not correct, for numbers are derived from the ideas themselves, not the ideas from the numbers, as Aristotle seems to suggest in his *Metaphysic*. Aristotle's ideas, not always in sympathy with those of Pythagoras, tend to the belief that the Pythagoreans were so full of numerical ideas that they changed everything into a number. Everything with them, says Aristotle (*Metaphysics*, xiv, 5), ideas, injustice, separation, mixture, and even man and the horse, were all numbers. He even suggests that the number was the very being itself, which is, of course, absurd. For how can a number be a being, a horse or a man ? He must surely have understood the idea that all things progress and grow, and that growth is a *rhythmic* series of movements, and hence perfect and exact, so that when considered commercially and practically it comes to

be known as Arithmetic. Doubtless, in endeavouring
to combat the looseness of thought which comes
from an exaggerated idea of metaphysical things,
and to show the practical way, the scientific method,
he allowed himself to appear to ridicule these ideas.
He says, certainly, that, according to the Pythagoreans, heaven and earth were harmony and
therefore numbers, but Pythagoras, it is certain,
taught no such doctrines. What the Master did
teach is that "there is a mysterious connection
between the gods and numbers, on which the
science of Arithmancy is based. The soul is a world
that is self-moving; the soul contains in itself, and
is, the quaternary, the tetraktys [the perfect cube]."

Other writers also attack the Pythagorean teaching. Asclepiades, quoted by Chaignet, suggested
that it was not the impossibility of describing their
ideas that caused the Pythagoreans to use numbers
in this manner, but an instinctive love of mystery
and a leaning towards a secret knowledge reserved
for the élite. Scarcely a well-balanced judgment!
Moreover, as is well known, Pythagoras was not only
a master of the science of Nature, but a master of
the exact science of Mathematics also. Where these
two are blended there is little fear of error. The
Pythagoreans, says Chaignet, were fundamentally
physicists (vol. ii, p. 33), mathematics being but
the form through which they presented their ideas.
It was not, we may be certain, a love of mystery that
prompted Pythagoras to teach his science in secret,
as some have thought, but rather a knowledge of
human nature and of the peculiar reactions of the
human mind. He understood, doubtless, that too
much knowledge, offered to and accepted by a mind

incapable of grasping ideas clearly, tended to develop erroneous conceptions rather than an understanding of the fullness of the teaching. Hence, all teaching of a deeper nature must have been graded to suit the minds of those who sought knowledge. But men who do not realize that the very growth of the head may be forced by a too anxious or mentally greedy acquisitiveness, querulously demand to know why these matters should be hidden, and why all this mystery !

It should be noted that Pythagoras taught not only the science of Nature and of Mathematics, and the science of Life, but he specially explained his ideas with reference to Music also. Chaignet, speaking of his well-known system of music, says that it was, above all, "an arithmetic". If he had said that it was the "science of true rhythm", and, therefore, connected with the science of Nature, and even with mathematics, he would have been nearer the truth (see page 105, ii).

These terms—figures, numbers, music, and cosmic progression—are thus intimately connected, each expressing one aspect of the Reality which is beyond them all : God. "Harmonious proportions", says H. P. Blavatsky in *The Secret Doctrine*, "guide the first differentiations of homogeneous substance into heterogeneous elements."* And in this pregnant sentence is summed up the idea which it is intended to express and explain in these pages.

Since God's creation is a regular and definite progression, it may, in one sense, be said to be perfect, and God may rightly be considered as creating according to number and form ; and in

---

* *Ibid.*, 3rd edition, vol. iii, p. 436.

this sense He is truly the Grand Geometrician and Mathematician of the universe.

As far as can be understood, the Pythagoreans, and those who studied along such lines, used mathematics theoretically and symbolically as well as practically, and this, probably, because they realized not only the obvious uses of numbers in mathematics generally, as applied to merely commercial affairs, but also their deeper sense. Thus they learned to *think* in number, i.e. to consider realities in their progressive states ; and to these states they gave the names of numbers.

This method, as far as it is understood, is used herein, although it is not claimed that it is explained with sufficient clearness for all who read to comprehend thoroughly. Indeed, it is doubtful whether the complete knowledge of numbers will be explained in this difficult age. Many books have been written on the subject, but no one has as yet explained its fundamental realities, as signified by the phrase *theoretic arithmetic*.

Numbers, as has been said, relate in the first instance to cosmic creative processes, and in the last to human physiological pre-natal development. According to Pythagoras and his followers, Number is "the extension of energy of the spermatic reasons contained in the Monad. Or, otherwise, that which, prior to all things, subsists in a divine intellect, by which and from which all things are co-ordinated and remain connumerated in an indissoluble order. Hippasius sees Number as the judicial instrument of the Creator, and others as the 'first paradigm or manifestation of mundane fabrication'."*

---

* Taylor's *Theoretic Arithmetic* (1886), p. 3.

The writer of these pages, without other authority than that of reason, suggests that Pythagoras taught doctrines relating to the birth and growth of the universe, and that these doctrines were explained in secret because of the persecution from the adherents of the orthodox "state religion" which their proclamation would have invoked. Hence, when spoken of outside the Inner Circle, these doctrines were mentioned very guardedly, numerical symbols and strange descriptions being used to convey the ideas expressed by Pythagoras concerning the generation of the worlds, etc. Thus, God coming forth to produce a universe was called *the Monad* or *One* ; for although this name was seldom applied to Jupiter or to the Supreme Being, the students knew of it in that connection, and hence the *One*, to them, represented God as Creative Cause, or Essence.

Cornelius Agrippa states that Nature was primordially formed by the ideas behind numbers, and that from these, in turn, arose the quality of the elements, the revolutions of time, the movement of the stars, and all the heavenly changes. Numbers have, he says, very great virtues and powers, and are at the root and base of all things.* This is, of course, in line with the doctrines of Pythagoras, whose followers speak of Number in the rational, rather than the material, sense.

The Christian Fathers were, also, assured that there was an admirable and efficacious virtue hidden in numbers. Agrippa mentions SS. Jerome, Augustine, Erigen, Ambrose, Gregory, Athanasius, Basile,

---

* *De Occulta Philosophie* (1533), book ii ; now published under the title *La Philosophie Occulte*, by Chacornac of Paris, 1910.

Hilaire, Rabunus, Bede, and several others as conforming to this idea, and Hilaire states that the Psalms were put in order by the Seventy by means of numbers. Rabunus, says Agrippa, wrote a book on the virtues of numbers, but the book is, unfortunately, undiscoverable to-day. It is probable, however, that such writings were for the most part more or less "magical", and no improvement on the Pythagorean teachings. At present there seems to be no book extant on numbers the teachings of which cannot be traced back to Pythagorean sources.

The remarks of Proclus on the teachings of Pythagoras and Plato concerning the One and the Many are, like his commentaries, too involved and intricate to be considered here. The reader seeking this deeper philosophy will find it in Book II of *The Six Books of Proclus* (1816), translated by the Platonist, Thomas Taylor.

It may, however, be said that Proclus states that the *One* is the principle of all things, and is transcendent ; it is not in itself divided, although it causes division in all things ; remaining the same throughout, it permeates them all. This is also the Hindu conception of the Supreme,* and has its corollary in the Christian doctrine of Immanence and Transcendence.

H. P. Blavatsky, in *The Secret Doctrine*, shows that numbers have very deep meanings, but she gives little information suitable for the ordinary reader and leaves much to the intuition of the student. She says that one represents God as manifested Deity, i.e. the "one" which issues from the

---

* *"Having pervaded this whole universe with one fragment of Myself, I remain."*—Bhagavad Gita, x, 42.

"no-number", the Circle Potential. She does not explain the number two, but says that the three represents Father, Mother, and Son, or the triangle. Number four she describes as a "female" number (i.e. an even number) and the root of illusion, the first solid figure being the quaternary, the Pyramid. Five she refers, among other things, to the Pentagon, symbol of the thinking, conscious man, and hints that it refers also to "Mind" in the universe, though she does not make the suggestion entirely clear. She shows the five as sacred with both the Hindus and the Greeks, when referring to creation. Number six is the symbol of Venus, reproduction, or the "spagyrization" of matter by triads. Number seven is the number *par excellence*, having all the perfection of the unit. Eight is the symbol of the eternal and spiral motion of cycles, symbolized in turn by the Caduceus; it shows the regular breathing of the Kosmos presided over by the Eight Great Gods— the Seven from the Primeval Mother, the One and the Triad. Nine, she says, is the triple ternary, the third reflexion of that number which reproduces itself incessantly under all shapes and figures, in every multiplication, and symbolizes our earth in its undeveloped state. "Ten", she continues, "brings all these digits back to unity." As the One and the Circle, or Cipher, it represents the Absolute All manifesting itself in the generative Power of Creation.

But perhaps the best description of numbers ever given is contained in the recently published and extraordinary book, *A Dictionary of the Sacred Language of All Scriptures and Myths*. "Numbers", states the author, "become symbols because the internal universe is on a definite and co-ordinated plan in which quantitative relations are repeated correspondentially through different states and planes. . . . One is the initial number of the Monad, the centre of all things. Two represents the inevitable duality of being on the plane of manifestation. Three represents completeness of state, the perfect number of the higher planes. . . . Six also represents completeness because it adds duality to three", i.e. a duality of a denser development, a *duality of trinities.*

It is interesting to note in passing the idea that to number or to cipher is to make a form, i.e. to create and make manifest. Gerald Massey states, in this connection, that the words *Cipher, Cyfr, Chiffre, Sifron, Zephiro,* and the Hebrew Sphr are all derived from an Egyptian word, *Khefr,* meaning *to figure,* or *to make a form.* The famous Egyptian beetle, *Khephra,* the Scarab, emblem of the reforming principle of Nature, was so called because of its power of rolling food into a ball (a cipher or figure), *Khep* meaning *to form* or *to fashion.*

It should be noted in conclusion that there is a certain danger incurred in the study of the lore of numbers which cannot be exaggerated, although it will not be easily understood save by those who have experienced the result of such study while morally unprepared. The power which the student may sometimes draw into himself when trying to realize the inner meaning of these great names and powers is sometimes so great as to cause a physical breakdown. There comes a moment when it seems as if an abyss of knowledge stretches out before the student, and in outstretching his arms to clutch what he sees before him he frequently overbalances and falls into the pit. In extreme cases the end is insanity. In milder cases a slight mental trouble may easily result.

So it will be understood that a first-hand acquaintance with these powers is not at all desirable save to those who have so far perfected themselves as to be prepared to receive, very gradually, the enormous flow of power with which they come in contact. Mental study of such a nature, without the corresponding moral upliftment, is disastrous, as is well pointed out by H. P. Blavatsky, who says :

The mystic characters, alphabets, and numerals, found in the divisions and sub-divisions of the Great Kabalah, are perhaps the most dangerous portions in it, and especially the numerals. We say "dangerous", because they are the most prompt to produce effects and results, and this with or without the experimenter's will, even without his knowledge. Some students are apt to doubt this statement, simply because after manipulating these numerals they have failed to notice any dire physical manifestation or result. Such results would be found the least dangerous : it is the moral causes produced, and the various events developed and brought to an unforeseen crisis, that would testify to the truth of what is now stated had the lay student only the power of discernment.

It is not, however, suggested that the metaphysical side of numbers is dangerous ; the danger exists rather in relation to the magical side, especially if studied for personal gain.

In this work, however, it is the *spiritual* side of ⟨ numbers which is under consideration. This being considered the fundamental aspect, practically no attention will be paid to the "magical" side of the subject. It should nevertheless be remembered that in addition to the arithmetical use of numbers, and the metaphysical conception of Number, there is a magical side which cannot be ostracized from a fuller study of the subject. A knowledge of the inner reality and power of Number gives rise to many exceedingly curious speculations, such as fortune-telling, character-reading, and the like ; and although this lower side of the science of Number is founded on fact, it is regrettable that it attracts all too many who seek knowledge for personal gain. It is this side of numbers which brings its votaries into difficulties. It is fundamentally certain, but there are few who understand it at first hand, and so have to fall back upon books on the subject, the writers of which but copy from others and seldom give a true reason for their affirmations.

The arithmetical use of numbers, wonderful, almost miraculous, as it is, is but a faint reflexion of the true Inner Reality behind Number, that Reality, the Rhythm of the Universe, which reflects itself unerringly in the science of Mathematics.

Fundamentally understood, Number is Rhythm. Unless this is borne in mind the study of Number may well be fruitless. Such a study, pursued reverently and without selfish ends, does not seem to bring difficulties in its wake. And since it is the purpose of these pages to treat rather of the deeper and theoretical side of numbers than the practical and arithmetical, it is necessary to realize that numbers, in the deepest sense, represent Cosmic and Creative processes. They represent states of a performed act from the ideal conception to completion of the constructed form in which the Idea is to dwell, i.e. the states that range from the potential zero to the completed 10. They are the rhythms of the universe, and show its emanation or production from out the depths of the boundless and illimitable space which is God "in the beginning".

It is hoped that the reader who considers the explanation set forth in this work will thereby understand the fundamental reason for numbers. Thus he will know exactly why any particular number used in the science of Numerology means what it is said to mean by the professors of the art who merely affirm, but never explain. Here follows, then, the explanation so far as it has been possible to the writer.

CHAPTER I

CREATION BY NUMBER

THE fundamental reality behind the idea of Number can only be accurately understood in its relation to and connection with the emanation of a universe, or of other lesser creative acts of God or man. Such, as has been seen, is the true Pythagorean teaching; indeed, the Pythagorean system is impossible of entire comprehension unless it is primarily understood in relation to Number. With its help, however, the deeper meaning of numbers and their names becomes clearer, and it is more easy to understand exactly how they represent the growth of a universe. Though they may be applied and understood in connection with any conceived plan carried to completion, it is with this evolution of a universe from a so-called "nothing" to which attention is especially directed.

It might help towards a swifter comprehension of the matter if it were permissible to coin new verbs from the names given to numbers. Thus *to one* is to be potential, individual, ready to go forth and begin a work; *to two* is to polarize oneself from one's idea, to differentiate life from substance, to pass from the stage of *one-ness* to that of *two-ing*, or, in other words, to polarize a one-ness and make duality. *To three* would mean, in this sense, to attract the "opposites" thus polarized, so that from the interaction all numbers or offspring might be developed. *To seven*, in like manner, means to consummate, to complete the unfoldment of Unity; and, in a sense, to return to the place or condition of starting, i.e. to make a cycle of accomplishment by means of the interaction of one and two to their full capacity in a series of progressive movements.

The idea of polarization, or *two-ing*, can be seen in the illustration of the man and his idea. Undifferentiated from the man himself, the idea is useless; he has, as it were, to become aware of the idea, to be conscious of it as separate from himself; his mind must become as a mirror in which the idea is reflected as a picture. Then only can polarization ensue and creation commence; the man, his idea, and the means by which he makes it known,* the link between the two, forming the first human trinity.

Since, then, the true meaning of numbers can only be fully realized by understanding cosmic processes, it will be necessary in the following chapters to offer an explanation of these processes. In this explanation the reader will notice that all the ideas relating to Number have placed against them in brackets the special number to which each such creative act or rhythm refers. Thus it is said "God causes polarization", and the figure (1) is added to show that it represents God as causal Unity. The (2) similarly placed shows that the act to which reference is made—polarization—is that to which the number in question is related.

Before proceeding further, it will be necessary to

---

* The building he erects, the book he writes, or even the child produced by interaction of the two.

have at least some idea of what is called "the Creation". Naturally, there are only ideas and concepts to be considered, for there are no "authorities", and the pure reason is the only guide the student can safely follow. In the opinion of the writer, the ideas here set forth are those held by the Pythagorean school, those on which were based the meanings they applied to numbers. This will become clearer as the study proceeds.

The conception of the Absolute, the All, or ⊙ Potential, is difficult of comprehension. Moreover, the idea of an abstract "hidden Father whom no man hath seen at any time" is not a satisfactory one, for man demands, and indeed needs, a God with whom he may, as it were, enter into relation. Therefore it seems that God is manifested in a creation in order that He may be realized through a focus of matter, i.e. through the worlds He produces. In this sense, God is only known as His workings in matter are observed (1). He, it may be said, puts Himself down into the worlds He "creates", "limits" Himself that we may more easily reach Him, more easily comprehend Him through His finite manifestation (1), and eventually realize through Him That which is the Infinite All (⊙).

This focusing of Himself is a help towards a slow and gradual realization by humanity of His reality. An absolute, incognizable essence is inconceivable to man, but an "individualized" God, if the term be permitted, is more satisfying to the human mind, which, by its inherent nature, cannot merely be content with concepts, but demands facts. Thus, God, it may be said, gives Himself an Individuality (1) by voluntarily circumscribing His Life within the system He produces, "the One in the Nought", the potential 10, or completely *manifested* Unity. This means that the human mind comes to realize that if worlds are visible, an Intelligence must be working through them, guiding and sustaining them during their evolution. The existence of these worlds is the "fact", the thing accomplished, through which the Idea, God, is realized. "Fact" and Idea thus become one, and God is known by and through that which He produces.

This, as far as it can be explained here, is the Idea of the Logos in the Heavens, the manifested God, or "Word" made flesh, God's Life voluntarily crucifying Itself (1) on the "opposites" or Cross of Manifestation (2) ; it is the *Cosmic Christ*, God's own Self.

Illimitable Space Itself, the "nought" potential, being the All, and therefore infinite, has, of necessity, no beginning, for a beginning can only be posited of that which is finite. This cannot be proved in the sense that ordinary facts are proved ; it is not a "fact", though it is none the less true ; it is a concept, that which is taken into, and conceived by, the mind. A fact is an appearance, a thing accomplished (*facio, to make* or *to do*) ; it is a phenomenal appearance behind which lies the Idea that produced it. This Idea is the reality, the noumenon. The fact is only cognizable by reason of the reality which gives it form and makes it manifest. A concept cannot, therefore, be treated as if it were a fact.

To grasp this conception of the non-beginning of the Infinite, it is necessary to understand the varying terms used by philosophers. The word *existence*, the term most frequently employed, is used to describe the Reality we call *God*. Even the greatest thinkers endeavour to prove the "existence" of God, by which they mean that God *Is*. Again, God is spoken of as Substance, especially by Spinoza, whose concepts are almost perfect, although his terms certainly appear misleading. *Existence* and *Subsistence* are terms used in these pages, as is also another less frequently met with, viz. *Persistence*. Hence a definition of these terms will be necessary.

"Existence", from *ex* and *sisto, from* or *out of*, and *to make to stand*, is obviously that which "stands out" or "appears". Hence to say that God exists is not correct if the literal meaning be accepted, for that which appears or stands out must necessarily stand out from, or within, some Reality; must appear within, or stand out from, the All as if it were an epitome of the All, a "reflexion" of It. It cannot be said to be Infinite, since it is but an appearance.

Hence, if, as Spinoza proves, and as is here accepted, God is Infinite, then it cannot possibly be said that He *ex-ists*, though it may be said that creation is a manifestation of His power; and it is this creation, this manifestation, which "stands out" in Space, and is known to be finite, having a beginning and an ending, as is proved by the observation of astronomical phenomena. It is this which is here spoken of as existence.

Yet it may be said guardedly that God exists, in the sense that He Himself manifests through the system He produces; but the idea is not clear, nor specially accurate, for though God may truly be said to limit Himself by producing worlds and confining Himself within them, the fact remains that God, considered as the All, is Infinite, and therefore does more than merely *ex*ist—He *per*sists.

For some reason, the word "persistence" has not been much used by philosophers, yet it is not a term easy to reject. The word is derived from the same root as "existence", viz. *sisto*, meaning *to cause to stand*, the prefix *per* meaning *through*, and the two conjoined giving rise to the conception of that which "stands" or endures through all things, which is beyond and before as well as after ex-istence. It thus may well be related to that which is called the Absolute, the All, that which ever Is, which has no beginning, although within it beginnings and endings take place. This state of Being, although itself without circumference, may be symbolized by the cipher o.

In the word "subsistence" there is again the root idea of *standing*, added, however, to the prefix *sub*, meaning literally *under* ; the whole meaning *to stand under*, or that which stands under, the background, as it were, of Existence (2).*

God, therefore, is the One, the All, illimitable, ever-lasting, That which ever is, ever was, and ever will be, That which Persists, lasts through and through. In this sense, "He" is not "a" creator, but is that in which creation arises. The All, as the All, does not create ; it is itself uncreate and can do nothing to make itself more or less, can produce nothing save that which is already within Itself as a possibility. This is what underlies the idea of *Persistence*, the absolute Reality in which all things appear and seem to disappear, in which, as has been

---

* The reader will find it helpful to refer occasionally to the later chapters dealing with these figures.

said, all things "live and move and have their
being". It is the o potential, That which persists
before all things, and into which all things are
finally resolved.

The usually accepted idea of creation by God
as a magical act, as the production of a universe from
nothing, is based upon a mistaken interpretation
of the words, "In the beginning God created the
heavens and the earth". It is hoped to show in
a later volume that this weird dogma would never
have arisen had the Book of Genesis been properly
understood. Such an idea as the creation of a
universe "from nothing" is as ridiculous as the
pseudo-scientific explanation of existence as the
result of a "fortuitous concourse of atoms".

God, then, as Totality, is Infinite, whereas
"Creation"—i.e. that which is manifested, which
ex-ists—is finite. The one is Persistence, the
"nought" potential; the other Existence (1 and 2).

Persistence, then, is a nonconditioned, unmanifest, uncreated Reality which stands beyond
all things. It is "Space", the All, before anything
tangible or objective is produced therein. Such
a concept necessarily involves the idea of what the
human mind calls "nothing", inasmuch as it relates
to Space with, apparently, nothing within it.

But before worlds are "created", before any
material thing appears in Space, there is God, Unity,
necessarily containing everything possible, everything that is to be, within Himself. God is the
Great Potentiality. God persists. God Is. Yet
only by the creation of worlds, of forms, can He
ex-ist, can He show Himself. Herein lies the
difference between Persistence and Existence. It

is the form which exists (2) ; the Life (1) behind
the form subsists. For existence, something must
appear from within the One through which He may
manifest. Before, or rather beyond, that all is
Persistence, for when existing forms and worlds are
again resolved into the Oneness, Subsistence and
Existence become once more unified as Persistence.

Before studying beginnings, therefore, it is
necessary to consider That in which they take place.
That is God, as Absolute Persistence, as we have
seen. But if forms come into manifestation, if
worlds appear in Space, there must be within God
that from which He produces the Substance of
which the worlds are formed, i.e. this apparently
empty Space, the o potential, God as Abstract
Potentiality, must contain within Itself all the
potentialities which are later to be viewed as
actualities, as things seen, things manifested.

One of the potentialities of God in His aspect
of Persistence must, therefore, be Substance—His
own Substance out of which He causes matter to
be produced. For if forms and worlds exist, there
must not be only that which sends them forth, but
that also of which they are materially composed.
Thus, although God is Unity, if He chooses to
show Himself forth and ex-ist in and through His
"creation", there must be a state as of Duality—
God's Self as Life, and God's Self as Substance (2).
He is thus both Energizing Force and Root-Substance. But it should not be forgotten that these
two are really one, that only for purposes of creation
is the Unity to be thought of as Duality.

Thus, no manifestation is possible while God
remains Unity ; manifestation, or creation, neces-

sarily implying the idea of Something working on Something, for instance, God (1) creating by means of His own self-sameness, His Substance (2). For purposes of creation, then, there exists that condition which science calls polarity, and which may well be termed "two-ness". A good illustration of this is as follows :

A circular piece of steel, complete and unbroken, is magnetized. Iron filings are brought near to it, without result. The circle is then broken, and what is called a "horse-shoe magnet" is formed. This broken circle, or horse-shoe magnet, shows two poles, one active and the other passive, and the power which was put into the circle by magnetic touch or stimulation now shows itself forth by means of these two opposite ends, or poles. Acting one against the other, they cause the inherent power to manifest, so that when iron filings are again brought near to it, the magnet attracts them. Thus the unconditioned, the circle, had within it two opposite powers, positive and negative, which remained unmanifested whilst in a state of balance : only with the breaking of the circle could they become active.

Here is an instance of that which is at the same time both Unity and Potential Duality. Used as a symbol of that which occurs when God wills to manifest, it should explain the processes symbolized by the 1, 2, and 3 subsisting potentially in the nought. In this sense, God may be thought of as the Unbroken Circle containing all things within Itself, all active and receptive powers, Spirit and Matter. Unmanifested, God is an unconditioned Reality, a Persisting Whole ; and before He can

manifest, can show Himself forth in and as a
Universe, a polarization must take place in this
unconditioned Reality. Thus a duality appears,
"spirit" (1) and "matter" (2), the latter being in
a very deep sense God's Existence, and the Life
sustaining it His Subsistence. Yet the Three are,
it must be remembered, in reality One ; it is only
the human mind which sees the Unity as a Trinity.
This Trinity is the first and ideal Trinity, the only
real and true Idea of which all other Trinities are
but densifications or reflexions.

To consider the All as the All, i.e. as absolute
or unconditioned Reality (God as infinite, or
boundless and illimitable Space and all that is contained potentially therein), is to think of God as
Persistence. On the other hand, to consider the
visible, manifested worlds, and realize the power
within all things, is to think in terms of duality,
of the Universe as seen and the Life beyond and
within it.

This apparent duality must, then, be defined
as Existence and Subsistence. God, as already said,
cannot be said to *ex*ist, in the strictest sense of the
term, in spite of Spinoza, unless the worlds be considered as God, on account of their birth from Him.
It is more correct, however, to speak of God as the
Whole, the Persisting Reality.

It will be noted that the word "Subsistence" is
here used in two ways : one to describe That which,
as Life, pervades all forms, which sustains and
stands under all things ; the other to describe the
Root-essence of Matter, which is called Substance
because it is the root of matter, or *stands under*
matter.

Thus, as Unconditioned Reality, before Time was, God persisted as an unbroken "circle" containing all potentialities, as ⊙. But it is obvious that the worlds and forms now in existence must have had some derivation ; therefore the idea of a persisting root-cause for Matter is posited, and this root-cause is called *Substance*. Similarly, the Life which is within form must have persisted as Life before creation. All things were in the Unity, both material Base and efficient Cause.

It is as if, before Time was,* this infinite Reality willed to show Itself forth, to embody Itself, and so by Its Will polarized Itself (2) as *This* (1) and *That* (2), God as God's Self, and God as God's Substance, or Spirit and Matter.†

Within "Space", then, *before* Time, this existing Substance (2) was everywhere, and with it God, as Life (1) ; the two, Causative-Essence and Formative-Substance, Father-God and Mother-God, a Unity, interacting by polarity to produce the worlds. This great Unity may be imagined as an infinite Ocean, the "Deep" of Space, an ocean of invisible, substantial and plastic stuff, within which, as an integral part of Itself, or its very nature, was that Life which had sent it forth.

Through Space, everywhere outspread, was this ocean of plastic stuff, this untouched *virgin* substance, this "sea" or cosmic flux (2). The ancients well symbolized it by the term *sea* ; for water is ever changing in form as it is moulded to its containing

---

* This is not to say "in the beginning", for the Absolute has neither beginning nor end, and is continually manifesting and "resting".

† Or Substance, that Æther out of which Matter is formed or woven

vessel, and is thus a fitting symbol of the plastic substance from which all forms are to be made. Using the Latin word, this *ocean* of Space becomes the *Virgin Mare* (the same word as our "Mary"), the Mother-Substance of the whole universe.

God and His Substance are One, therefore He is one with the *Virgin Mare*, the pure matrix from which spring all things. It is, as it were, a part of Himself, His *Sister* or *Wife*, in a strictly metaphysical sense. Yet since God works within it to produce the worlds, and "comes forth from it", within the worlds produced, to ex-ist in and as a universe, He is, symbolically speaking, the result, and, hence, the *Son*. In and through that Substance or Mother-Stuff which is in reality Himself, he works, and comes forth into manifestation (4); and in this sense He is, symbolically speaking, not only *Father* but *Son* also, *His own Son*. The Mother-Stuff, the *Virgin Mary*, is, in like manner, *Wife* as well as *Mother* to her own *Husband*. These relationships, however, must never be interpreted literally, and certainly not anthropomorphically!

Father, *Mother*, and *Son* are thus but aspects of the One Reality, and it is from the fundamental Idea of these that later conceptions seem to have arisen, conceptions which, arising in the minds of people who did not understand the Reality behind, became "facts" so-called—as if they were to be considered "geographically and not ourano-graphically", to use the strange words of Thomas Vaughan. In this sense, as aspects of the One, "no one is greater nor less than another", *Father* (1), *Mother* (2), and *Son* (4) being equal and, indeed, the same.

The idea of the Holy Ghost (3), which is mentioned where the *Mother* is practically ignored, is not easy of explanation, but the illustration of the magnet may again serve to explain this also.

The unbroken circle, containing within itself positive and negative poles as possibilities, symbolizes God, who contains like potentialities. But in this unbroken Unity lies the power (3) which causes polarity, or duality, the power which makes the Unity to appear as a Duality, and which, when the duality appears, draws the opposites together, and permits of a relation between them. It is this power which, even in the cell, divides in order to unite and form new bodies, divides but to attract together the parts which really are one. The same power now makes zero (o) manifest as Trinity.

Thus the two "opposites" emanate from a common unity in which both powers of opposite-ness were held in abeyance, balanced in solution. Polarization strikes this balance and divides the one-ness into opposites. In each of these, however, is the same unifying force as was in that from which they sprang; and though separated and made into apparently different parts, and maintaining their integral differences, they yet seek to unite with each other.

This affinitizing, polarizing, separating-and-drawing-together power is the "power of the Holy Ghost"; it holds together all parts so that the Unity can never be actually broken.

It is well known that when a piece of steel is placed across the poles of a horse-shoe magnet the power ceases to act, i.e. manifestation ceases, and the "three" once more become "one", and in quiescence await the opportunity to come forth anew and recommence activity. Thus the unbroken circle and the horse-shoe magnet are fitting symbols of that which is before the emanation of a universe.

In this "aerial" ocean of cosmic substance (2) worked the Life (1) of God, the "spirit of God moving over the face of the waters". If, however, instead of using the word "waters" the word *Chaos* be used, as it was with the ancients, the idea is the same; for this unconditioned substance with its latent possibilities of becoming, as sketched very guardedly in Genesis, is the same as that of the Greek myth. Though understood in one way by the Greek populace, the real meaning was clearly known to her philosophers, as Elton's translation of Ovid clearly shows :

> *Ere earth and sea and covering heavens, were known,*
> *The face of nature, o'er the world, was one :*
> *And men have called it Chaos : formless, rude,*
> *The mass : dead matter's weight, inert and crude :*
> *Where, in mix'd heap of ill-compounded mould,*
> *The jarring seeds of things confusedly rolled.*

It should be noticed that it is not the earth, our little globe in space, of which mention is made, the poem dealing with That which was before the earth existed. This shows that the Greeks held that there was originally an unconditioned, spatial Ocean, a flux of Substance, which existed before the universe was formed.

Over this confusion, according to the Greek myth, ruled the god *Chaos* and his consort *Nux*, or Night. This is equivalent to saying that "darkness was upon the face of the deep", night and darkness being similar terms and symbolizing the same states. Night was, then, upon the face of *Chaos*, and the two ruled together. Then *Erebus*, literally *darkness*, their son, was asked to assist his parents ; but instead, he dethroned his father and married his mother, so that Night (*Nux*) and Darkness (*Erebus*) ruled together. From this "iniquitous" union came two beautiful children, or "opposites", respectively named *Æther*, or Substance, and *Hemera*, Day or Light. These two in their turn seized the ruling power, and together "illumined" space by their radiance. They asked their child to help them to produce the worlds, to make a Cosmos from Chaos, and *Eros* (lit. *desire to create*) polarized substance and produced further "opposites", called, in this case, *Earth* and *Sea*.

Eros is thus the symbol of the polarizing force which divides to bring together again. He is, of course, the same as Cupid, the piercer of hearts, the great affinitizing power of the universe ; and is also to be viewed as what some thinkers have called the "second aspect of God", i.e. God as the Sustainer of His universe, as that Love which not only holds the universe together, but is also responsible for individualizing (separating) the parts. In fact, it is stated that *Eros*, being called to help in the great work, "pierced" the earthy substance with his arrows and vivified it, i.e. polarized the substance itself. This, coming after the polarization by *Chaos* and *Nux*, thus symbolizes the second polarization, of which mention will be made later.

In the Buddhist traditions, this polarizing Force is almost personified as *Fohat* (3). This Being may be regarded as the Force which causes the relation and interaction between all such powers of opposites as are of a common unity; it polarizes (2) a unity (1), and, having done so, it brings the individualized parts together for purposes of creation.   It links and binds all atoms, forms, and beings together, differentiates matter, separating whilst unifying all things.   *Fohat* is, in fact, the Buddhistic equivalent of the Holy Ghost, and of the synthetic power personified by the Greeks as *Eros*.   In all cases, it is the Divine, Energizing Force which works in Substance to vivify or link (3), bring forth and make manifest (4).

In the more ancient Hindu traditions we find the great sage Manu* propounding the Laws and Ordinances, beginning with an account of the emanation of the worlds.   The ideas expressed, although a little obscure in translation, are the same as those held by many philosophers.

This [universal diffused substance] existed primarily in the shape of darkness, unperceived, destitute of distinctive marks [undifferentiated and without qualities] unattainable by reasoning, unknowable, wholly immersed, as it were, in deep sleep.   Then the Divine Self-Existent, indiscernible, making This [the substance in question] the great elements and the rest discernible [manifest], appeared with irresistible power, dispelling the darkness.

The words in brackets are not present in the translation of Buhler, but are introduced here for the sake of clarity.   In Sanskrit, of course, the word here translated "darkness" is *Tamah*, which means

---

* *The Code of Manu (Sacred Books of the East.* Bühler).

much more than mere darkness, and refers in fact to everything which is inert, sluggish, dark, resistant ; it is the opposite of Mobile. In another sense, Darkness is that state in which, or from which, we look for something to come forth ; it is an unknown quality, an *x*.

The Hindu tradition also states that the Creator, desiring to produce, created with a thought the "waters" of Space and placed therein the seed which became the golden egg from which He Himself was born as Brahma, the manifested Progenitor of the world. These waters are known to the Hindu as *Narah*, or the Supreme Soul-Substance, and He, Brahma, is called Narayana, *the Mover on the Waters*, in exactly the same way as God is spoken of in our own Scriptures.

These varying teachings may be summarized as follows : Before time was, God as Logos (1), or Manifestor, projected Himself as (or into) the ideal Substance (2) of all things, and was Himself immanent in that ideal Substance. This Substance, this infinite ocean in Space, was unconditioned potentiality, all things being held in it as in solution, until God's vivifying power (3), *Breath*, or Holy Ghost, prepared it for polarization by brooding, as it were, over plasticity, generatively working within or "over" it. Then God "said" let there be a polarization of Substance ; and there broke forth the *Light*, the Divine Spark which "exploded" this unified element and prepared it for purposes of existence.

Thus, "In the beginning God created the heavens and the earth."

D

CHAPTER II

THERE is, as will be shown, no idea in this work of the ordinary orthodox sense of a creation of something out of nothing. The idea here accepted is of an emanation or sending-forth of a universe from a persisting Root-Substance which "stands beyond or under" the various degrees of matter as known.

Now, the word "create" comes from the Latin *creo*, which has been accepted as meaning *to create*. This is obviously no translation or explanation, but merely a repetition of the word *creo*. The real meaning of the Latin word, the idea behind it, its essential nature, has still to be discovered, and it must be admitted that this is not easy. Certainly *creo* does not come from any root meaning *to make*,* for the Latin equivalent of *to make* is *facio*, which means *to form something from a given substance already in being*, an idea clearly visible in its derivatives *fashion* and *fashioning*, which connote the shaping of something from an already existing substance, whether material for a woman's robe or a robe for Universal Mother Nature. *Creo* is not, then, a word meaning *to make* or *to fashion*, and therefore its real signification must be sought elsewhere.

---

* It may, of course, be from the Sanskrit root Kr, *to do*.

Although it is not here affirmed that all words are derived from the half-human, half-animal sounds made by some savages and children, yet the opinion must be expressed that some words undoubtedly arose in that manner. Language has grown in various ways, and difficult though it must inevitably be to prove that many roots are descended from "sound-language"—i.e. from roots which by their sound express the Reality behind them—nevertheless the attempt has to be made, for it is a part of that logical reasoning which, taken in its entirety, constitutes proof—proof, that is, for those who will to understand, who are willing to consider not merely facts, but concepts also.

The theory of sound-language is that the true name of a thing should, and originally did, express the quality shown forth by that thing. In earlier times names were given with knowledge and understanding, and the thing named was therefore called by its proper title. A name was thus *sign*ificant, was a sign or a sound indicative of the real nature of the thing to which it was applied.

A study of the word "creation", or *creo*, will help to make this concept clear. The root-sound is RA, or modified as BR. In the Hebrew word translated *create* it appears as BRA, and in the Sanskrit as Brih. The Hebrew sound-picture, the letter B, or *Beth*, means literally *house*, and was originally written to represent a house ; it connotes some condition from which something is expected to come forth, as does a house, that in which there is both life and movement. It is therefore symbolical of that from which all matter is produced, the "house of God", or the *Sub*stance which is with

God, which is part of God's nature. As helpful in this connection, it should be noted that the sound Bé, or B, is not so much forceful and outward-going as inward and assimilative—a sound, in fact, as of interior preparation.

Reish, the next letter of the root BRA, is the symbol of Intelligence,* whilst the third letter, A, called in Hebrew *Aleph,* or Bull, is essentially as well as symbolically the sign of Power. Conjoined as BRA, these letters form a word meaning "an inner preparation by directive Mind, and a sending forth by power". The translation of this root as *to create* is therefore not quite accurate, since it does not represent the making of something from nothing but a coming forth, an emissive rolling out from a primordial Root-Substance, an evolutionary development.

As translated in English, and accepted by orthodoxy, the word bears many interpretations, and is used to convey the ideas of *to produce, to make, to create, to form,* and even *to bring forth,* though it must be obvious that the word does not cover all these meanings and the processes they indicate. Certainly in the Sanskrit the idea is more clearly expressed ; the name given to the Creator, *Brahma,* from the root *Brih, to expand,* is much more correct than the English interpretation as the creation of something from nothing. *Brahma* means literally "He who expands Himself, who sends forth His own substance from which to produce the worlds", the idea which also underlies the Hebrew root.

Yet even in the word "create", or *creo,* of which it is a derivative, the same underlying meaning can

---

* Its *sound* denotes a directive Energy.

be sensed, and even heard, in the *sound*, although the C gives a harsher touch, as if expressive of both internal assimilation and forth-going. In both these roots, BRA and CREO, *Berrar* and *Kerrar*—a hint as to their correct pronunciation—the same emissive, rolling sound is to be caught, and though each is modified by its suffix and prefix, they remain radically the same in essence. In *Creo* there is the idea of Power and Intelligence working actively in its depths to produce ; in BRA the same idea of Power and Intelligence workingly inwardly to produce.

There is thus very little real difference between them, and each root may be said to signify what we call creation, or, better, emanation. The same sound may be caught in many other words also, as in that used by the Hindus to describe God as Producer, i.e. Ishv*ara* (*pervader*), in that used to describe God as Cause, *Bra*hma ; in our own words *bring*, *birth*, *born*, etc., and in *cre*ate—all of which signify a coming forth, from something or somewhere, of that which was already in being and had to be manifested or "created". The word "breath" is, perhaps, even more expressive than any other, and in the phraseology of some Eastern philosophies God, symbolically speaking, "breathes" and the worlds appear. He withdraws His breath and they cease to be ; a very striking and significant simile.

Such, then, is the idea here accepted of what is generally called "creation". It is a preparation (1)* of the "field of manifestation", or, rather, of the

---

* The reader should note that the numbers in brackets represent the processes here described, as already explained.

Ocean of Cosmic Substance (2), within which will eventually arise the many "little islands", or atoms, from which groups called worlds, but literally great islands in an Ætheric Ocean, are formed.   Creation is *a rolling forth, an emanation* (3), *after a polarization* (2), *and preparation* (1) of That in which it arises and from which it comes forth (⊙).

The word "creation" can never be proved to represent the actual making of something from nothing.   The process is not a *making*; it is a preparation for production, a preparation which necessarily precedes the "fashioning" symbolized by the figure 5.

The word "production" is from the root DUX, *a leader*, or DUCO, *to lead*; the preposition *pro* meaning *forward*.   The whole word thus implies *a leading forth*, and represents the second aspect of the Creative Trinity.   First there is the preparation of the Substance, then it is made manifest, is "led forth", as it were, to be "fashioned" into many grades of matter, and atomized for the building up of worlds, bodies, and forms of all kinds.

The word "fashioning" is the only one in the trinity of Creation-Production-Fashioning carrying within it the idea of making, though even here it is not the making of something out of nothing. The word is from the Latin *facio, to make*, and is obviously used correctly in English in the sense of shaping something from a pre-existing substance. It can be applied, as already stated, to the idea of fashioning a robe of woven material for woman, or a Robe of Matter-Stuff for Mother Nature.

In a previous chapter it was demonstrated how, when polarization of the Oneness takes place, what is called duality arises, and two "opposites" "come forth", appearing as Subsistence and Existence, or Causative Life and Formative Substance.

The same idea has now to be considered with regard to Substance itself. Had this remained undifferentiated, then there could have been no resulting formation of atoms, worlds, or forms. But just as Duality was contained in solution within the One, so within the oneness of Substance was contained a power of becoming many different kinds and qualities of matter. Hence there was required a further polarization. The Life, which is God, being everywhere in this Substance, polarized the oneness, with the result that there arose different kinds of matter (6). Thus we have solid matter, liquid, gaseous, and the finer ethers of which science now has knowledge ; and even finer matter must be postulated if the Cosmos is to be considered as a whole.

God's Life, then, it may be assumed, polarized this Root-Substance in the same manner as the original polarization was effected. Exactly how it was done cannot be thought, much less explained ; but that it has been done is obvious, since manifestation is impossible unless in matter there are different grades. That they are here now proves that they have been produced, and it is therefore logical to imagine them as inherent "qualities" in the original Substance. Had these "qualities" not appeared there would be no existence, for a Oneness remains Itself—simply *per*sisting. *Ex*-istence demands an apparent duality, an appearance as of opposites (2) ; there must be one quality of matter working against another quality, for it is only by opposition and resistance, or even friction, that the universe of form can be "created".

Life being presumed everywhere in Substance, hence the opposite qualities of Substance will, by their nature, show forth the qualities of the Life (6). Thus if two kinds of matter are derived from the one Substance by polarization, the one acting against the other whilst yet being drawn to it, they may well be distinguished by calling one kind *this* and the other *that*; or, if more definite descriptions are needed, they may be described as *fiery* or *active*, and as *earthy, sluggish, inactive,* or *inert*—the opposites having directly opposite properties.   But there is a third quality, which, being formed from the same One Substance, has relations with each opposite or tends to bring the two together in itself; this other quality may be termed *blended, rhythmic,* or *balanced*.   These three—the two opposites and the middle quality which makes relationship between them possible—are a manifested Unity, a polarized Unity, every polarized Unity being a Trinity when existent.*

This Substance, which is posited as being the base of God's operations, is at first a primary, unconditioned Unity; it is not chaos in the sense of dis-order, but chaos as pre-order.   Certainly the translators of the English version of the Bible are not correct in stating that it was "without form and void".   Without form it undoubtedly was, but not by any means void.   It was a fullness, a great potentiality, containing within itself all things which have since come forth.   It was not a chaotic

---

* The metaphysical student will see in these qualities the *Gunas* of Indian Philosophy.

nothingness, but a fitting base of operations, plastic and formative.

The great Hebrew grammarian, Fabre D'Olivet, gives the Hebrew terms quite another signification. He states that the Hebrew THU VaBHU represents not a void and formless substance, but a Substance extending almost to incomprehensibility, almost to annihilation, and exceedingly fine. He gives his own translation, and says that this Stuff was, as it were, a germ in a root, or, as he quaintly expresses it, "*Une existence contingent et potentielle, renfermée dans une autre existence potentielle*". This, as will be seen, is the exact essence of the idea here presented. D'Olivet's phrase, however, is one which will repay much meditation, and should be specially useful to those who prefer to think things out for themselves.

Life, then, considered as Force, must of necessity show itself in opposite ways. If Life goes forth but does not return, if it is, that is, unlimited, then there can be no production of forms, no manifestation. But if Life rushes through Substance and returns to itself, a "shape" or abode for the Life is formed. Force is essentially unity, but it must act in a dual fashion, going out from a given point (centrifugally), and pressing back towards that point (centripetally). Thus the Life, spreading itself abroad, in and through Substance, has the power, as it were, of checking itself in order to prepare forms. Meditation will show that this apparent limitation is a necessity for purposes of existence. But for this duality, this limiting of itself, Force would never become definite, and would merely continue in a forward and indefinite manner.

without an end and therefore without achievement of purpose.

But a force thus polarized to work through matter will necessarily act as if it were a trinity of Force (6), for any polarized force shows forth not only two distinct opposites, but also a state between these, a neutral zone in which the two are, as it were, blended (3). This third quality may, perhaps, be likened to a state midway between motion and rest, an intermediary stage in which the opposites are in sympathetic relation with each other.

If, then, we consider Causative Life and Formative Substance together, we see that wherever Life is in its three aspects, there it will manifest Itself through Substance. Therefore the ensouled Substance will answer to Force, i.e. the "below" will reflect the "above", and show forth like attributes (6). Substance is impressed, as it were, with qualities caused by the trinitized Force working within it ; in it arises (5) matter of different qualities, and from these different qualities of matter the worlds (10), atoms (7), and all things are fashioned.

It is, then, the "Divine Spark", the fiery energy of God, which, in polarization, exploded or disturbed the equilibrium of the mass and prepared it for manifestation, or, in other and more orthodox words, "God said let there be light, and there was light". God said, "Let light, the polarizing Force, be manifest", is but another way of expressing the same idea. It should here be noted that this "light" is not the light of day, for the sun had not then been created.

Another illustration, interesting to students of chemistry, may here be given. If oxygen and hydrogen in certain proportions be collected in a bell-jar and blended as one, this jar will obviously contain a dualized substance, invisible, yet present. This substance, although unseen, certainly does exist, just as the Substance of substances, equally unseen, had its being in Space before the emanation of the worlds. Now, before this gaseous substance in the bell-jar can be polarized to create, certain preparations are necessary : the two must be separated, even though they are bound, by affinity, to rush together again. To this end, a lighted taper is introduced, and an explosion results ; the gases separate, and in rushing to merge themselves again they form water—a new substance, and a denser, and yet one of which the constituent elements are the same. This phenomenon illustrates helpfully the concept of polarization and affinity, or "threeing".

Now, if an electric spark be sent into dynamite placed beneath a material structure, this material structure, which is a kind of composite unity, will be broken up or "destroyed". This is the making of an end to previously existing things. But if, before existence, before "creation" and the building of forms, the "divine dynamic spark" arises within Substance, it may well prove itself a force in many ways akin to the other, tearing, rending, and disintegrating to destroy the unity but only in the sense of preparing it by polarization for creative purposes.

The effect of this Power will be to force apart substance from substance, to produce different qualities, or grades, in order to build. This is the real beginning of things (5), somewhat analogous to the end of things.

Thus the Law of Polarization seems first to separate any given substance into parts, and then to draw these together again. So it may be said that here is again duality—polarization before creation becoming afterwards affinity.

The result of this polarization of substance by the "Divine Spark" was, as has been said, the production of different grades of matter which, though actually the same essentially, were set free to act as if independent of each other. As parts of the Unity in which both had arisen, there was in each the tendency to return to the common source, a tendency held in check by the polarization that had given to each its independence. The affinitizing force, unable to draw them back and cause them to lose their particular integral quality, drew them together in order that they might act one upon the other, to blend, and mingle, and give to each other separately the quality created by that union. And just as the mixture of gaseous substance in the bell-jar illustration gave birth to a "new" form of matter, i.e. water, so through the polarization of Substance by the Divine Spark, a "new" matter, derived from the old, was formed—matter which, though partaking of the original substance, is yet different in its way of manifesting.

It is perhaps the first time that this action of God's Mind, or "the Spirit of God moving on the 'waters'", has been described as sending forth the spark of polarization, yet to call the essence of God's focused "Mind" a *Spark* is not new, rather is it a tradition of the ages. Prometheus, as is well known, was said to have stolen fire from the gods and given it to man. He was the personified bringer to man of that mind which makes man grow as "one of Us". It is the Divine Spark of mentality which makes of the human animal a thinking being ; and it has to be introduced into the body of man, or, rather, *educed* from within him, in order that he, too, may be polarized, may be separated, in a sense, from the body, the better to function through it, and to realize himself as a self-conscious, thinking entity.

The mind is thus likened to a "spark" because of its nature ; it is not, of course, really fire, but it is akin to fire in its workings ; it is, as it were, bound up in the body, in the nature of the Life, but when some great being such as Prometheus, *the before-thinker*, "fires" the brain into activity, it is as if the vital spark introduced stimulated into activity the previously latent capacity for thinking.   In like manner, also, the presence of more highly developed beings than ourselves among us stimulates the mind in man, causing it to rush forth from quiescence to potency, from the indefinite to the definite, from static to dynamic activity.

It is the nature of fire to destroy all things in its escape from the material in which it has lain latent, and just as this inward fire contained in all things rushes forward to mingle with a spark of fire applied from without and thus cause a conflagration, so the mind in its uncontrolled and dynamic condition tends to tear and rend all that comes in contact with it.   Like fire, it can both destroy and create.

The necessity for this polarization of Substance becomes obvious when the indispensability of limitation is recognized.   Without limitation, universes, worlds, forms, individualized parts of any kind, are an impossibility.   If there were an absolutely illimitable creation, i.e. creation without limit, it would merely resolve itself into one-ness again, and become a flux instead of an existence.

This same idea has to be borne in mind when the next step in creation, viz. atomization, is considered. To prevent "fluxing", to prevent matter melting back into its primordial, unconditioned oneness, finite particles of matter, atomized matter, are required. This atomizing process is symbolized by the number 7, as will presently be seen. Spinoza vaguely suggests the idea of polarization in his *Ethic*, prop. 32, wherein he speaks of the attributes of God—Motion and Rest—from the interaction of which all things have their rise. This concept is not difficult of understanding in the light of what has been said. It may also be explained in considering human attributes. If, for instance, what is called *Will* is at work, it must have some resistance against which to fling itself; that is, there must be opposition; and this implies opposites, in this case the sluggish, inert body and the fiery, active mind and will. In like manner, the Will in the universe works in Matter and is opposed by the Resistance which also works in Matter ; the one, fiery and active, is in opposition to, and opposed by, its passive, inert, resistant opposite.

Everywhere in Space, then, previous to creation, there was a mass of undifferentiated Substance, and this mass had to be prepared for production and fashioning. To this end, the balance of the whole was disturbed by the dynamic energy or "Will" of God, and from this relationship arose the different qualities or grades of matter. Just as the rainbow is caused by a breaking-up of the original "white" light into primaries and a septenary, seven colours from the pre-colour or "white", so, by analogy, we may presume the original Substance as being broken up for creative and formative purposes.

The resultant qualities do not, however, actually separate matter into distinct and separate parts ; the whole remains a whole, though "coloured" by the qualities imparted to it ; it remains a oneness, though the power which has caused the qualities to arise prevents their rushing into each other and losing their individuality. Yet the power of polarization allows of free intermixture, and quality blends with quality in mutual relationship. Only polarization could produce this consummation.

God and His Substance are one, and as He is not only the All, but is also everywhere, it is reasonable to imagine Space as filled with an "Ocean" of plastic stuff—Æther, as it is called by the Greeks. However modified by the Power within it, this Root-Substance was a flux, a "solid" mass like unto water, from which nothing could be built until it was atomized. Before this process took place there were no distinct "drops" in this plastic "Aerial Ocean", just as there are no distinct and separate drops in an ordinary ocean. All Substance, therefore, was atomized, built up into distinct portions of which each was, as it were, "a" life in a separate covering of form.

Symbolically speaking, God "breathed" into the Ocean of Substance, and this creative breath, or force, which was dual, literally pushed back Substance in the same manner as air in water pushes back water and leaves "bubbles". Each water-bubble is an actual atomized portion of air in water ; in each there is a space which is a vacuum as regards water, but a plenum, a fullness, as regards the air within the space. Similarly, when God "breathed" into Substance, the ensouling breath, or Force, rushed into the empty spaces formed by pushing back the plastic Æther. This Force, though a oneness, yet works in opposite ways as if it were a duality. The inherent power of "outward-going-ness", that power which is called centrifugal, is unable to act indefinitely, as it is held in check by its opposite, the contractive, centipetal force. It rushes out in space, but can proceed only so far as the "will" of God, the dynamic energy behind the whole, permits, and when that point is reached it must return to itself.

For instance, if the purpose in view is the production of atoms of a certain degree of complexity, the Force sent out by the Divine "Will" will be inhibited by a "thus far and no farther", with the result that when that limit is reached the stream of Force turns back upon itself, and in turning leaves behind it atoms, individualized portions of Life surrounded by a wall of substance, like bubbles of air in water. The globular, spherical atom we know is the natural result of such a dual force. A figure cannot, of course, be formed by a straight line, or even by a curved line ; but if the Force pushed out returns to its place of starting, it will necessarily tend to produce a form which is spherical. This formation of atoms is, then, the "sevening" process.

All is now ready for definite formation (8). Matter has been produced, qualified, atomized and separated, each part from every other part. But the whole is *one*, one Substance, and truly incapable of actual division, just as an ocean remains an ocean, a oneness, despite its so-called "drops". A difference, however, does exist, for whereas drops of water have no distinct individuality, the atoms of Substance, or Æther, are distinct—distinct for the purpose of fashioning the forms in which the universe is to appear and ex-ist. So that, although there is no actual separation of Substance and the atoms can only remain atoms while God's Power or "Will" holds them to the "thus far and no farther", the whole is yet definitely atomized for purposes of form-building.

At this stage the actual building up of a universe (8) begins. This is the consummation of the work, and is symbolized by the number *seven*, leading ultimately to the completion represented by the *ten*.

Let us now turn to a consideration of the Cosmos Processes symbolized by the numbers one to ten, and follow, step by step, the development of a universe (10) from the Infinite Reality (⊙).

E

CHAPTER III

THE reader will by now have realized the idea behind the theory here presented, namely that creation is by "number", or, rather, rhythmic progression, and that this can be seen in the study of any creative act, whether cosmic or microcosmic, universal or human.

In the beginning, before creation, there is the X, the Unknown Quality, the Absolute, the Great Potentiality. All powers and all potentialities are in this Absolute,* but whilst It remains inactive creation is impossible, since nothing can exist whilst It remains unpolarized.

This Unconditioned or Unknown Quality may be symbolized by the figure or cipher ⊙, within which is placed a point to represent Potentiality and to show that the circle is not barren. The o is used in arithmetic to represent "nothing", and also, when added to other powers or numbers, to represent all things. Without this symbol of "nothing" multiplicity cannot extend beyond nine. Therefore it may well be said that this Circle Potential, this ⊙, is the first number in the cosmos, and is symbolic of the Unknown, the Illimitable. It contains all *numbers*, i.e. all possibilities, within itself,

---

* The Absolute may be considered as the Grand Totality, or even the Totality of a Solar System which is the absolute to the human mind.

just as the light of the sun contains all colours in its "whiteness".

For purposes of creation, the Cosmic Point of Potentiality becomes active, and from it arises the First Power in the Universe, that Power called by some *God*, or Logos, by others *the One*, and by the Pythagoreans the *Monad*.

Now, Production, or creation, implies Polarity, or the existence of "opposites" within the Unity. Production cannot take place without this polarity and the resulting interaction of the opposites thus produced, as is seen especially in the case of Colour, being evident also in Music.

Thus Light itself is pure white, which is not a colour, but a solution of all colours, as black is negation of colour. This pure white, this beyond-colour or colour-cause, shining through a prism, is broken up into seven parts, each of which is a distinct and primary colour in itself, although all seven are "one" behind the veil. Thus, if there is a veil of water, a rainstorm, between the sun and the earth, the white light of the sun is broken up in passing through this veil, and we see a rainbow.

Thus, just as the white light is colour unmanifest, colour *in posse*, so also in the Absolute all qualities and forms are held as in solution, needing the Divine Spark or "Word of God" to call, or send, them forth into manifestation. By reason of their common unity, their fundamental oneness, there is naturally a tendency in the three primary colours to coalesce, to come together, and these three as pigments produce, in their interaction, seven. Thus, red and blue rush to combine, blue and yellow, and yellow and red, also, which gives six colours from the

primary three. The seventh colour is that wherein
all are equally blended, a colour which is practically
a blue, an indigo, an intermediate stage, not even
sufficiently definite to be called a colour. The
same is seen in Music, *Fa* being the intermediate
stage, or note.

As with Light and its manifestation as seven
colours, so with the universe and its manifestation
as seven *numbers*, or stages of appearance. But to
explain the qualities shown forth by the different
aspects of Absolute is not easy, for they cannot be
seen : they can only be sensed or intuited. The
adoption of the symbolism of colour may, however,
prove helpful to some.

In Colour, the first place is taken by the fiery
red, the positive, overpowering, glaring state which
seems, like a king, to place all others in the shade ;
in fact, although many prefer the more suave and
gentle blue, red is the Ruler, despite that all do not
approve his rule. In Matter, also, the dominating
quality is of a fiery nature, and in Sanskrit is actually
called by the name given to the Ruler, viz. *Rajah*,
or *Rajas*, the Ruler being supposed to show forth
the dominating quality of *Rajas*, which may be
compared, as a correspondence only, with the "red"
quality which emanates from the white light.

Now, the active, dominant quality presupposes
the existence of an opposite quality which is neither
active nor dominant, and a third quality produced
by the interaction of these dominant-inert opposites.
Thus we may think of the three primary qualities
of Creation : as the Positive, the fiery, active type,
the one ; its receptive, inert opposite, two ; and
that which, different from either, in some way

partakes of both, and, being a state above their separated condition, is well called *rhythmic* or balanced, three. These numbers may thus be related to Matter as well as Spirit.

The gnostic Marcus, misquoted by the heresy-hunter Irenæus, states, according to Mead :

Before all universes there is a source before the primal source, prior even to that state which is inconceivable, ineffable, unnameable, which I number as Noughtness. With this No-numbers consubsists a Power to which I give the name One-ness.*

The reader will note the similarity of this idea to that expressed above. The o, or zero, is truly before all that exists, and contains within Itself the potentiality of all things. It is, however, passive, and needs vivification or fructification to produce. Hence the *One*, the Point, which becomes a line, enters into relation with the o to bring forth all "numbers", all Rhythms ; and from the association of these two all Cosmic processes spring.

---

* *Fragments of a Faith Forgotten*, p. 373.

CHAPTER IV

THE NUMBER ONE

THE Greek term *Monas*, or *Monad*, is generally used to describe unbroken unity, or, as it is sometimes called, *One*. Taylor, in his *Theoretic Arithmetic*, states that Archytas or Philolaus spoke indiscriminately of the *Monad* or the *One*; the best Platonists, however, when referring to "divine natures", speak of the *Monad* as that which contains distinct, yet profoundly united, multitude, whereas one was "the summit of the many", and therefore more simple than the *Monad*.

According to this definition, the one is an individualized and distinct part of a whole, the first of a series which does not exist unless followed by other "numbers"; while the *Monad* is that which includes all "numbers", holds all division in check, a wholeness, an Absolute.

This idea of one as the "summit of the many" is interesting, and shows that it is the beginning, or apex, of things, all numbers spreading out from it, and increasing, until a base is reached (as *Ten*).

Taylor* seems to think that the Pythagoreans, in using the names of numbers to describe the creation, or generation of things and of their cause, did so only symbolically. Indeed, although the best exponent of the Pythagorean teachings, Taylor does

---

* *Ibid.*, p. 164.

not seem to realize that the fundamental basis of numbers is *Rhythm*, and that on this Rhythm the generation of all things was based.

Numbers are, as already stated, the names or descriptions of Cosmic Happenings and Ideas. These Ideas, when reflected in dense matter, come to be known only as they are applied to utilitarian and commercial matters. But it was the Cosmic Happenings at which the Pythagoreans hinted, though no one seems to have been permitted to give the full explanation.

When speaking of the *Monad*, or the *One*, the Pythagoreans referred to that which is before creation ; to them it was a symbol of that which was complete, undeveloped, and unevolved. The philosophically minded among them called it *Primordial Chaos*, and the religious *God*, but both understood that the terms applied to the same thing.

According to the different authorities quoted by Taylor, the One, the Monad, or Primordial Reality, that which *is* before all things *appear* and after they disappear, was named, by the Pythagoreans, *Intellect*, *Male and Female*, *God and Matter*, *Chaos*, *Confusion*, *Obscurity*, *Darkness*, and *Atlas*. It was also said to be *recipient*, and "capacious of all things" ; and was further called the *Sun*, *Pyralios*, or *Morpho*, *Tower of Jupiter*, and *Spermatic Reason*.

Now, the One as a numeral, or *commercial* value, when added to the odd makes it even, and when added to the even makes it odd ; hence the Pythagoreans, when considering the *One* as *Idea*, looked on it as containing all things within itself, inasmuch as it partakes of both natures, the so-called odd and even. And if for these latter words, spirit and matter,

or creative and receptive, be substituted, the meaning
is clear.   Spirit may be called "odd", *causative*, or
positive, inasmuch as it acts on and enters into relation with matter, which is "even", or receptively
formative ; and this, the One, entering into relation
with Matter, gives rise to all "numbers", all rhythmic
progressions.

This *Monad*, or "first number" of the Pythagoreans, is equivalent to that which, in modern language,
is called the *One*, a distinct and active Potential
Energy.   But in the science of theoretic Arithmetic,
or *Arithmosophie*, as Dr. R. Allendy calls it,* the
words *One* and *Unity* have by no means the same
meaning.   Unity is the All, That† which Is, whether
there is a Universe and Individual Beings or not.
Within this Unknown Illimitable, the *Advaita*, or
"One without a Second" of Hindu philosophy, the
One, the "First Number", arises, and is the "creator"
or "cause" of all "numbers".

Within this "Circle", in which all things live and
move and have their being, arises, for the production of the worlds, the "Point Potential", the
"Individualized" Being called God. This, to students
of symbolism, is signified by the statement that the
"Point" of *potentiality* becomes, for creative purposes, the "Line" of actual Being.   In other words :
before creation, there must be identification, and
this necessitates what is called individualization.

Thus the one is the first of those rhythmic
happenings in space which are called *numbers*,
or *numberings*, i.e. identifications.   It is not Unity,
but the beginning of Diversity. As Dr. R. Allendy

* *Le Symbolisme des Nombres*, p. vii.
† THAT is the All-Inclusive Reality of Hindu philosophy.

says, when speaking of the All, the Circle Potential, "Unity is not, properly speaking, a number. . . . It constitutes the irreducible root of all ideas of number . . . a pure abstraction . . . only considered as *one* conventionally", being in reality "the All".*

One, on the other hand, is that which is distinct and, in a sense, separate from all that which surrounds it. It carries within itself the first Idea of Individuality in the deepest sense of this much misunderstood term—that is to say, it is not an actual and distinct separateness ; it is distinct only in the sense of acting creatively in an individual manner. It remains one with the All, just as a family is a Unity, whilst the individual member is one.

The Infinite, this Unity, is not bound, for the All is illimitable ; it is not distinct from others, for there is nothing but Itself. Yet it includes all, and hence is beyond that which is called one and described by the term *individuality*, for individuality implies a following, a *second*, and the Unity carries within it the idea of no second : it is, as we have seen, "the one without a second".

Unity implies synthesis whilst one implies diversity. A union is a blend of numbers or divers things ; an individual one-ness is separative, distinct, defined. Singularity expresses the idea of individuality better than unity, for singularity is not unity. Unity is unification, the holding together of the divided onenesses, or individuals ; for unity includes in itself all diversity.

This difference between Absolute Unity and the definite one is seldom explained in modern writings. The Pythagorean teachings in regard to it do not

* *Ibid.*, pp. 1,2.

seem to have been expressed very clearly by writers on the subject, though it is beyond doubt that the idea was taught by Pythagoras himself.

This Monad, "containing distinct but profoundly united multitude", is what is here termed the All, the Absolute, God, or Unity, That which includes all numbers, even the One, within Itself. But the idea of "distinct but profoundly united multitude", though helpful to thought, is not exact, and it seems better to speak of the All as a Great Potentiality containing a power of becoming, a power of appearing as if it were many.

The idea that the one "is the summit of the many", the origin of all numbers, is seen in the Hebrew word for *One*, which is sometimes called *Achad* (*Unity*), and sometimes *Chad* (*One*), meaning *an apex, a summit,* etc.

Thus the power symbolized by the number 1 is the *Cause* of the making manifest of all numbers, and the symbol represents generation, as the figure used clearly shows. The 1, Life, in its relation to Substance (2), is the generator of all things and all changes, i.e. of all those rhythms called numbers. These, the one and the two, are primarily Spirit and Matter, or Life and Form, or God as Causative-Essence and God as Formative-Substance.

It is obvious that there cannot be creation without some kind of definition, and this naturally implies limitation even in a Creative Power. It follows, therefore, that the Creative Power itself is definitized and, in a very deep sense, individual, even though God is not a person.

In Sanskrit, the word used for one, viz. *Eka*, represents, according to its letters, a causative and

life-giving power (E), assimilated (K), defined, and
forth-going (A). The European *one, unus, ein*, etc.,
and the Egyptian UA, all represent an emanation,
or power of causing the passing from one state to
another, a Principiation, a definition.

In the Hebrew word *Chad*, or *Achad*, is seen the
symbol of Causative Power, or Potentiality of all
things and all numbers (A), diversity (D), held in
check, or solution (Ch). This shows how wonder-
fully the secrets of Nature were hidden in letters ;
and in this case they themselves tell us what
Unity is. The root of the word, ChD, refers to the
top of a pyramid, to the apex, that from which all
things emanate. The whole refers to diversity (*D*),
held as it were in solution, held back (*Ch*) by power
potential (*A*)—a perfect definition of Unity.

The translation of the word as *one* is, however,
scarcely broad enough, or sufficiently expressive,
for, as its letters show, it represents Unity. The
definition of the Hebrew letters, however, explain
Fabre D'Olivet's reason for describing it as representing "division arrested, subjugated by a sort of
effort, as indicated by the two signs D (*division*)
and Ch (*effort*)", governed by the sign of potential
power.

The Unity is thus the All, the Absolute. The
One, the "first number", is, on the other hand, the
causative and generating power which is a potentiality
of the All ; it is the essential Life which has to
become individual and singular ; it is the Dynamic
Energy, the creative essence of everything, of God
and of man.

There is a widespread idea, translated from some
of the Pythagorean writers, that odd numbers are

good and even numbers bad ; but this is meaningless if taken in a literal sense, except perhaps as used in geomancy, or fortune-telling by numbers. The actual meaning is, of course, that the ideas represented by the odd numbers are active, positive, dynamic, etc., whereas the states represented by the even numbers are, in a deep sense, receptive, passive, contingently potential, etc. The states represented by even numbers need the active or odd numbers (the unpaired number) for their further development.

It is not certain that the Pythagorean teachings with regard to this subject were known to the ancient Chinese, but in the *Yi King*,* a magical book the origin of which dates back more than 4,000 years, and which is perhaps the oldest work on numbers which has been traced, though it gives no explanation of numbers *per se*, it is said that odd numbers are light, and even numbers *dark* and represented by groups of circles instead of what are now called *figures*, or *numerals*.

In this remarkable work, the meaning of which has baffled all its translators, the number 8 is used throughout, the arrangement of the rods, or lines, used being always in eights. There are 8 × 8 of these hexagrams, the odd numbers being complete lines, and the even numbers divided, positive and negative, male and female. The use of the number 8 is rather obscurely referred to the idea that these lines arranged in hexagrams represent all manifested things in earth and heaven. God is also said to complete His processes in 8 stages.† Legge offers no

---

* Legge's translation. (*Sacred Books of the East.*)
† *Ibid.*, p. 425.

explanation of this connection, but the reader may gain light by reference to what is said of the number 8 in the following pages.

Incidentally, it may be noted that the well-known arithmetical 15 puzzle is also found in this ancient book,* which shows the numbers 1 to 9 arranged as a square, each line of which is equivalent to 15.

* *Ibid.*, p. 18.

CHAPTER V

THE number two, the Duad, was considered from
many points of view by the followers of Pythagoras.
It was termed *Matter*, the cause of dissimilitude, the
interval between multitude and Monad; and it
was considered the fountain of all symphony, Erato
among the Muses, and also harmony and patience.
It was *a root*, though not a root in energy, for this
quality belonged to the One, and was called *Isis*,
Nature, *Rhea*, the Mother of Jupiter, and the fountain of distribution.

All these terms are characteristic of Matter, or
Substance, and symbolically describe its powers
and qualities. It was called *symphonic* and *harmonious*
because of its plasticity; *Nature* and *Isis* because
it was the Mother-Substance of all things. But
inasmuch as Matter is resistant and obstructive, it
was also called *ignorance*, *falsehood*, *difference*, *strife*,
dissension, *Fate*, and *Death*. It was considered as
feminine, obviously because it was the matrix of
all things, and naturally receptive and formative;
and was known as *Cupid* and *Erato* from its desire
for union with Spirit, or the *One*.

Two thus signifies *division*, *difference*, *Root-
Substance*, that which is polarized, from which all
existing forms, however rare, however fine, are
fashioned. The Sanskrit word *Dvi* (*Two*) expresses

by its sound this idea of polarization or division; indeed, the letter D and its sound is everywhere significant of the idea; and the derived words, *two, zwei, duo, deux,* all express it in their sounds, as also do the words *division, difference, difficulty, danger, divergence, dispute, duality,* etc.

The Hebrew term for two, *ShN* or *Shy-ni*, represents distinction and becoming, that from which, by energizing motion (Sh), all things are produced (N) and made manifest (I).* The same word is also used in the Egyptian hieroglyphs, viz. *SN* or *Sen-nu* (*Two*), meaning, as a word, *those which are like,* hence *Sena,* a brother.

It will be noticed that ShNI contains the Yod or I, the symbol of manifestation, in place of the potential sign A, and that to this is added the Shee-un (Sh), emblem of relative duration, and the Nun (N), representing augmentation and extension, and having the special property of spreading out. Growth, therefore, is the purpose of polarization or division as symbolized by this number two. It is also a symbol of "crossing", a term which is, by the way, the French word for growth, *accroissement.* The Cross, too, is a well-known symbol of the duality of things; for two is the opposite of the One. Whilst the One holds all things in *potentia* and in check (as shown by the letter Ch, the very sound of which is a deterrent), the chief function of two is growth.

In one sense, all numbers are derived from the One, yet, as St. Martin states in his posthumous work, *Des Nombres,* it is impossible to produce

---

* All Hebrew letters have exterior and interior meanings as well as sound-value. See the author's *Book of Genesis Unveiled.*

Two from *One*.* Hence, Duality is considered the actual beginning of manifestation, the One (Life, Essence, Being, or God) being co-equal with the two (Substance, Matter, or Form).

The human mind is incapable of realizing Life apart from form, even if such an idea could be posited. Hence the first stage of manifestation which can be realized is polarization, a drawing apart, as it were, of the Life-God from the Substance-God.

One multiplied by one gives nothing but one; hence the one needs the two, Life needs Substance, for manifestation and multiplication. Thus one, entering into relation with two, gives rise to three. Or, in other words, Life, ensouling Substance, becomes linked (3) to it, after having been polarized (2) from it (1). Opposites are essential for any creative purpose whatsoever.

The idea that duality is, in a sense, the first number, is confirmed by Cornelius Agrippa, who says that the dual number is the first number because it is the first multitude, and is the common measure of all numbers, or, as Pythagoreans term it, a confusion of unities.

For creative purposes this differentiation is necessary, yet duality is, in the deepest sense, an illusion; it is not a for-ever persisting Reality. The Reality is the One behind all opposites, the blend from which they spring.

"The error", says Dr. R. Allendy, "consists in taking an apparent and relative differentiation for an irreducible opposition and in misunderstanding the true Unity in which the opposites are founded."†

---

* *Ibid.*, p. 18.
† *Le Symbolisme des Nombres*, p. 31.

But, as will be presently seen, there is no absolute duality, no real or lasting opposition, between matter or substance and the Life ensouling it.

Much is to be learned from a deep study of this number. When that which is called the one, the unit, begins to permeate and produce a universe, a kind of opposition is necessitated, for without such contrast as is supplied by opposition there cannot be manifestation. Hence, God as the One, the Producer and Cause, polarizes His unity, draws, as it were, apart from His Substance, and then vivifies it. Thus arises a possibility of *ex*-istence, for it is Life in Form which alone makes "creation" possible. The One is, therefore, potentially dual, for, single whilst unmanifested, it thus reaches that state of potential duality which leads to Its duality in manifestation.

This law of polarity is the rule in all manifested things, and finds its expression everywhere : in the magnet, in the sex-opposites, in Sun-positive and Moon-negative, in Past and Present, in Present and Future, in the Matter and Form of Aristotle, in Subject and Object, Subsistence and Existence, Spirit and Matter, God as God's Self and God as God's Substance, in God the Father and God the Mother, in action and resistance, good and evil, God and Satan, and in all the innumerable "pairs of opposites" which are so well-known in the universe that they might well be termed the Scales of Life.

These pairs of opposites are not only necessary to existence, but constitute existence itself, inasmuch as the first and greatest pair of all is that from which no one can escape whilst in being—that of Spirit and Matter, Life and Form. But the would-be

F

perfect man has to learn not to allow himself to be thrown from one opposite to another, from one side of the Scale of Life to the other side. He must rise above the jurisdiction of the pairs of opposites, and himself become the Weigher of Things, balancing one against the other until he reaches the point of equilibrium, and thus rises above their power.

This duality, then, in a sense, is really the first number, a dual number ; within the Absolute All (here understood of the Monad, the ⊙, rather than of the one, the first number proper), duality has arisen, the resulting opposites being co-equal and, though in essence one, are but polarized opposites of or in the same Reality. Hence the first number, or that which is represented by the number two, is a pair, a polarized one. For purposes of de-scription, these opposites are *named* One and Two ; it is on these, on God as God's Self and God as God's Substance, that all manifestation, all existence, is based.

When the Monad, the All, is called the One, the duality arising within it may be justly described as an emanation from or showing forth of the One ; but since in these pages the Monad, Unity, is called the Circle, or Nought Potential, the polarized opposites, Life and Substance, arising within it, are spoken of as *One* and *Two*.

That these two are one in essence is obvious from the terms applied to them, i.e. Spirit and Matter, Life and Form.

Amongst the many strange expressions used by the followers of Pythagoras to describe the Monad as God, the All-Inclusive Reality, was that most curious definition : "Intellect, God, and in a certain respect, matter."

Taylor, quoting this, says : "They very properly denominated it *'in a certain respect'* and not wholly matter, from its similitude to divinity. . . . Hence matter is said to be dissimilarly similar to divinity. It is similar so far as it alone subsists by a negation of all things. It is dissimilarly similar because divinity is better and beyond all things, but matter is worse than and below all things."

This is the conventional view which seeks to understand realities and yet is bound by ecclesiastical formulas ! It is better to see God as Spirit and Matter, both in, and as, One. The one is no more divine than the other, for the two are but opposite poles of one and the same Substantial Reality, one showing forth its Dynamic, and the other its Static, nature; one being thus causative and the other formative; one active, the other resistant or receptive.

Dr. Allendy states that this duality "is, in fact, the static base in which may be deduced the essential dynamic unity [the One] incognizable in itself",[*] and the differentiation by polarity is the base of all cosmic manifestation. "The play of all the multiple individualities amongst themselves", he adds, is only possible "by means of the opposition of the agent and the patient, of the positive and negative, of force and resistance, of expansion and receptivity, of quality and quantity."[†]

This law of polarity works everywhere, in all natural phenomena—magnetically, electrically, and chemically—an idea which has the support of the Qabalists, who see everything manifested as male and female, in the deepest metaphysical sense. Even in the exoteric Hebrew writings such as Genesis

---

[*] *Le Symbolisme des Nombres*, p. 23.   [†] *Ibid.*, p. 24.

the idea is clearly expressed, as in the dividing of the "waters" from the "waters", which in this case represents the polarization of that Substance, which is the root of Matter—the "Waters" of space.

The idea that Spirit and Matter are essentially one cannot be proved scientifically, although the fact that Life (Spirit) is working in matter has already been demonstrated by ordinary scientific means. Students interested in this aspect of the subject would do well to study the works by Professor Bose, M.A., D.Sc., such as *Response in the Living and Non-Living, Electro-Physiology, Plant Psychology*, etc.* In these pages it is taken for granted that Life subsists in all matter. Proof must be sought elsewhere.

Since matter exists in such different states as solids, liquids, gases, and ether, it is reasonable to conclude that all are differentiations from the One Substance. Solid matter may be broken up into its component parts, the elements of earth, water, air, and fire. From the solid to the liquid, from the liquid to the gaseous, from the gaseous to the etheric, is one long unbroken line of continuity. Each type of matter may be resolved into the finer type above it, solids into liquids, liquids into gases, gases into ether, and these into a Substance which eludes the human mind and to which no description can be given. But what, it may be asked, is the difference between this invisible, intangible, and impalpable Substantial Reality and the Force, Spirit, or Life

---

* A simpler but comprehensive outline is contained in Professor Patrick Geddes' fascinating *Life and Work of Sir J. C. Bose.* (Longmans, Green.)

proved to be functioning in all matter ? Since matter can thus be traced to a state which is no longer material, it is not unreasonable to assume that its highest and primordial state is merely a densification of Spirit or Life, Matter being densified Life, and Life spiritualized Matter, the two blended as one being the Root Cause of both.

From this viewpoint, Spirit is no more real than Matter, and Matter no more real than Spirit, although Matter, as known, is resistant and limiting, requiring the utmost endeavour to escape its yoke. We find, as we free ourselves from the dominion of the denser grades, that the finer grades of matter assert their hold on us, and never can we escape from the domain of Matter so long as we exist as individuals, except only in an "inner" sense.

Thus there is One Reality, polarized as *Thesis* and *Anti-thesis*, actually a *Syn-thesis*, and beyond all a *Meta-thesis*, i.e. there is a Subjective and an Objective and That from which both spring.

What matters, therefore, whether it is said that in Matter is the promise and potency of all life, or that in Life is the promise and potency of all matter ? Such definitions are but words wherewith an attempt to express the Inexpressible is made, as if to measure the Immeasurable.

Quietly meditating, however, the student may touch That which is beyond all definitions because beyond all opposites, may himself contact the Self which is all things and in all things ; reaching beyond the phenomenon, the appearance, and contacting the sub-sisting noumenon, and thus know the Reality beyond both.

But why, it may be asked, do these opposites

exist if they are in reality one ? A valuable hint is given by Thomas Vaughan in his wonderful work, *Anima Magica Abscondita*, and will well repay meditation. Quoting an anonymous writer to whom the Brothers of the R(osy) C(ross) gave the name of *Sapiens*, he says, "Thou seest not that Heaven and the Elements were once but one Substance and were separated one from another by divine skill for the generation of thyself and all that is. Didst thou know this the rest could not escape, unless indeed thou art devoid of any capacity."

Vaughan further refers to the idea that Spirit and Matter are opposite poles or gradations of One Reality. "When I consider", he says, "the system or the fabric of this world, I find it to be a certain series, a link or a chain which is extended from (un)conditioned to unconditioned, from that which is beneath all apprehension to that which is above all apprehension . . . the Scala of the great Chaldee which doth reach from the subternatural darkness [Matter of the densest] to the supernatural fire [Spirit]."*

---

* *Lumen de Lumine,* ch. iii.

CHAPTER VI

THE NUMBER THREE

MANY of the great Hebrew philosophers of the Middle Ages seem to have been acquainted with the Pythagorean teachings with regard to Numbers. Avicebron (1021-70), of Cordova, according to Myer's *Qabbalah*, speaks of the affinity which exists between the "to be" and numbers. Three, he says, is the root of all things, because Form represents the Unity, and Matter the Duad, and these, with the Will, the bond between them, result in a Triad. "All existing things", he adds, "are constituted *after the nature of* numbers. . . . The highest Abstract God is the indivisible, metaphysical unity."*

Thus three, relating as it does to the interaction between two opposites and the synthesizing power which attracts them for creative purposes, is rightly considered the number of true beginning. It is the fundamental, mystic number without which no *production* is possible, for the One, though potential, can do nothing of itself, and the opposites are, in their turn, useless unless there is a relation between them, some synthesizing power which opens the way for development and growth. This is the power of the number three.

Gerald Massey states that the word "three" is

---

* *Ibid.*, p. 153.

synonymous with "tree", and that in many ancient languages the word used to represent this number represented also a power of production, growth, etc.

In Egyptian hieroglyphics, the word *Khemt*, three, means *to think out a matter*, i.e. *to produce it in the mind*, and this thinking out is itself a "three-ing" process, the result of interaction between the Man, his Mind, and the Idea. In the cosmic Process, God, Substance, and the Relation form this Trinity.

In the modern word "three", the sounds of the letters convey the ideas of a reciprocal (Th), energizing interaction (R), preparing for manifestation (I).   Fabre D'Olivet agrees that the sound of *th* represents reciprocity, literally *action and reaction*, between opposites ; and the idea is strengthened by its grammatical use in Hebrew, as in *Atha*, literally *thou*, which represents a being with whom *reciprocal* relations are possible, or, as Fabre D'Olivet puts it, "a co-existent being". The same idea is expressed even more clearly and simply in the English *thou*.

Tracing the word to its base, the Sanskrit *Tri*, we find, however, that it represents something prepared by motion (R), extended and drawn out (T),* and ready for manifestation, or that which grows and becomes, as in the word "tree".

The Hebrew word for "three" is *Shelishi*, which is spelt ShLUSh. This, according to Fabre D'Olivet's *Langue Hébraïque* (*Cosmogony of Moses*), is formed from two contracted roots : the first, ShL, representing every extraction or subtraction, and the second, LUSh, curiously enough, its opposite, viz. an

---

* The French *tirer, to draw out*, and the English *thread*, are interesting in this connection.

amalgamation, a kneading together. This is in perfect conformity with the idea that, as held by the writer, *Three* represents a mutual attraction between opposites for purposes of manifestation. D'Olivet logically concludes that the dual meaning of the word ShLUSh, i.e. extraction and subtraction united with amalgamation, shows that the number *Three* represents, under a new form, the opposed ideas contained in the numbers One and Two, i.e. the separation or extraction consequent upon polarization causes them to become "a kind of relative unity". Hence the *One*, Unity, passes into the state of Two, polarity, and becomes *Three*, a Trinity, when manifesting.

Every Unity must appear as a Trinity when manifested. Hence in many religions, either exoterically, or esoterically and metaphysically, the Trinity, which is always to the fore, is spoken of as the "Perfect number", i.e. the number of true beginning.

The opposites, being thus brought together, or "three-ed", a new power, the relation between them, is made manifest. Thus where the Three is concerned there is no hard and fast dividing line between the opposites, which now have between them a gradation made possible by the relation into which they have entered. Hence Day and Night, as absolute opposites, would be separated, whereas as a Trinity, Dusk, which relates to both, would be included.

Other trinities arising through a neutral centre, or relation, are : Male-Female-Hermaphrodite, Male-Female-Affinity, Past-Future-Present, Father-Spirit-Mother-Matter-Holy (Ghost) vivifying Force, Positive-Negative-Neutral, Beginning-End-Middle, the three Primaries in Colour, body-Spirit-soul, do-si-fa in Music, thesis-antithesis-metathesis, and the innumerable trinities which may each and all be considered as manifested unity. Each of these will, on examination, reveal itself as unity, unfolded into duality, and synthesized by gradation.

Dr. Allendy describes the action of number three by the words *organization, activity, creation, conception,* and *series*—words which express in the most concise manner possible all that has already been said in the foregoing pages, although his valuable chapter on the Ternary had not been read when these were written. The chapter itself is, however, so replete with knowledge of the number three that it cannot be passed in silence.

He states, when referring to duality as a *definite* opposition of parts, that there would be no possibility of reconciliation between them, since opposites and contraries can never combine for common action. Pure duality, if it existed actually instead of relatively (as parts of a whole), would be the negation of cosmic unity, and establish an abyss between the opposites impossible to span ; and this irreducible opposition would never cease to be sterile, inactive, and static.

"On the contrary," he continues, "the existence of an intermediary gradation, of a means of passage (a relation), between the two poles, makes their opposition fertile by permitting each to act upon its adversary and to receive the reactions."

When referred to as the Trinity, the number three represents the *Brahma, Vishnu,* and *Shiva* of the Hindu; the *Kether, Chochmah,*and *Binah* of the Qabalist ; in fact, it represents the three aspects of manifested Deity in all religions, as well as the three reflected aspects in the microcosm, Man. In other words, the One, represented by the Hebrew *Aleph*, or A, is the symbol of the Inner Self, the Principle, the Lord of all, whether of man or God ; it is the central pivot, the abstract principle of anything and everything. The second aspect, symbolized by the Hebrew *Lamed*, or L, represents an out-spreading, uplifting power, the wing of a bird (the Great Bird), and everywhere tends to extension and elevation. Grammatically, it is the directive article denoting reunion, and hence is used as a symbol of spirituality and Intuition in man. The third aspect, represented by the Hé, is symbolic of everything which vivifies, or universal life and the idea of being, and is therefore appropriately used to represent the receptive and lifegiving Substance, as is especially evident in the further meaning of the letter, *H* being used to emphasize and give prominence to things.

These three letters form the Hebrew name of God, ALH, or *Elohei*. When the Who, MI,* is added to them, that is to say when the "three-ing" stage is reached, the Elohim, the Seven Spirits before the Throne, are formed, and "creation" commences, as we see in the added letters, M and I, which, when added to the ALH, form ALHIM, otherwise Elohim. Now, the I, or *Yod*, is the symbol of manifestation, and the M, or *Mem*, represents the fruitful, formative side of Nature : therefore the Elohim made man androgyne, in Their own image, the Above always being reflected in the Below.

Thus the term *Elohim* is not a word in the ordinary sense, but a collection of symbols repre-

* The word *Mi* means *who*, and when reversed is a plural ending.

senting the process of *becoming*, of *emanation*. The A, or *Aleph*, is "parentless", and comes from the Absolute to help make complete, and to work through, manifestation on the lower planes. In the highest sense, the word *Elohim* is neither male nor female, singular nor plural, but includes all these opposites within itself.

It is interesting to notice in this connection that in Chaldaic the name of God is written as *three* Yods. These matters are, however, mentioned only in passing and must be fully explained elsewhere.

The Masonic meaning of the word "three" in the light of the Qabalah is of great importance, but has not hitherto appeared in public print save in an article from the pen of the present writer, which appeared as an editorial in the *Freemason*.

In the Hebrew word for *Two*, ShNI, there is but one *Sheeun*, whereas in ShLUSh, meaning three, there are two, showing symbolically that manifestation is more definite in the "three-ing" stage, as indeed it is when the Cosmic Mind comes into play. This is emphasized even more strongly by the addition of the *Lamed*, L, the uplifting power, which is linked to these two symbols of duration by the mystery sign, the *Vauv*, *U* or V, the link which joins and the point that separates. It is interesting to study the number three from the Masonic point of view, in connection with the five and seven, for in the roots of ShLUSh we have three distinct meanings relating to the three steps—extraction, subtraction, and amalgamation —which the pupil must take ere he can enter what is termed *The Outer Court*. His first step is to collect his forces together and prepare to learn ;

his next step to eliminate and subtract the gross matter, and his last to amalgamate, or synthesize, the result. This final step of apprenticeship gains for him the approbation of his master and leads him to a position in which he is enabled to grasp his work with his whole nature.

It is said in the Jewish *Book of Formation*, or *Sepher Yetzirah*, that the worlds were formed by *Sepher*, *Sipher*, and *Sippur*. One translator, Wynn Westcott, understands this to mean that the universe was created "by numbers, letters, and sounds" (!).

The word used in the Hebrew is SPhR, meaning *a book* or *a scroll*, but the same word, differently pointed, means also *a writer*, *a story*, or *a body of doctrine*. The word is thus symbolical of the fundamental three-in-one, of the three aspects shown by every manifested being, whether God or man. The Knower of things (the author) is identical with that by means of which he knows, and also with the thing made manifest thereby; therefore the Knower, the thing known, and that by which it is known, are one and the same.

In the teaching of the Qabalists and the language of metaphysics, the Subject, the Object, and the Instrument linking, or attracting, them are identical. Hence the word SPhR, meaning equally *Author*, *Book*, and *Idea*, was perfectly understood by the Qabalists, and when used by them expressed not only the threefold idea, but, by means of points placed below and above the consonants, whichever of the three aspects they desired to emphasize at the moment. The word was thus symbolic of world-emanation : the *Author* being God, the *Book* the

Sea of Substance in which, or on which, he operates to impress His *Story*.

In fairy tale and legend, myth and sacred story, in the Mysteries of old and the Lesser Mysteries of to-day, the number three is in constant evidence. In fairy tales there are always the three sons who go out into the world to seek their fortune, and it is generally only the third son who succeeds, and it is interesting to notice, especially in the light of the teachings regarding the "Three Outpourings" of God's Life, that this younger son, who alone succeeds, follows the elder two who go before him to prepare the way.

There is also the widespread superstition, as it is usually called, that a start in a race, or among acrobats, must never be made at once. The "one, two, three, and away" of the children's races is another form of the same idea, as is also the "turn round three times and catch whom you may". The idea of "one to be ready, two to be steady, three to be off" is curiously applicable to what happens at creation, the "one to be ready" being the Idea in the "Mind" of God, the "two to be steady" the sustaining of that Idea in Substance, and the "three to be off" the sending forth of the worlds into manifestation. And though it is true that such analogies should not be pushed too far, it will be found that there is generally something at the back of most "superstitious" ideas, and this idea of three attempts is no exception to the rule.

The different religious systems of the world practically all taught the fundamental Trinity. Even among the Jews the teaching is of importance, though there are very few of the orthodox who accept it to-day, on account of the materializing tendency which has, unfortunately, turned this metaphysical concept into a personal and earthly matter. The *Book of Zohar*, however, distinctly tells us that "three emanate from one : one is in three ; one is in the midst of the two which drew their sustenance therefrom" ;* and further : "the one in the midst, the link, draws from both sides".

The same idea, just as guardedly expressed, is found in Thomas Vaughan's *Anthroposophia Theomagica.*†

"God, the Father," he says, "is the Metaphysicall, Super-celestiall Sun, the Second Person is the Light, the Third is 'Fiery Love', or a divine Heate proceeding from both. Now without the presence of this Heate there is no reception of the Light, and by consequence no influx from the Father of Light. For this 'Love' is the medium which unites the Lover to that which is beloved and probably it is the 'Chief Daimon' who doth unite us to the rulers of Spirits. I could speak much more of the offices of this Loving Spirit but these are grand Mysteries of God and of Nature and require not our discusse so much as our reverence."

Thus this idea of a fundamental Trinity pre-supposes that condition which was before the worlds were created. This condition, symbolized by the Hebrew letters, *Beth* and *Reish*, the *House of Substance*, or Sea of Substance, in which was the Head (R) or *Motive Principle*, was, paradoxically, unconditioned, but, having polarized Itself, It gave birth to the *One* and the *Two*, and these, by synthesis and interaction, to the *Three*.

---

* *Zohar*, i, 32b.
† *The Works of Thomas Vaughan*, by A. E. Waite, p. 12.

CHAPTER VII

THE NUMBER FOUR

THE One having, in the deeper sense, polarized Itself, and having then become synthesized as a trinity, or triad, a foundation for all things is next prepared by the interaction of the synthesized opposites which have been conjoined or linked together by the Power symbolized by the number three. The rhythmic result is called four, and this number thus becomes the number of foundation ; and just as the triangle represents geometrically the idea of "three-ing", so the square is the geometrical symbol of "fouring".

The number three represents the approach of Idea and Form, the bringing together of the Thought and the Substance, the "three-ing" process characteristic of all creation, whether cosmic or terrestrial. The opposites having been thus brought together and synthesized, the next stage is naturally that of foundation, the "four-ing" process.

According to Gaskell's *Dictionary*, four is significant of system and order. Plutarch states, according to Gaskell, that it is by reason of this number that every body has its origin. This is, however, not to be understood as relating to the building of forms and bodies, which is the function of the Power of eight, but *cosmically*, i.e. of the preparation of the "stuff" from which bodies are fashioned, or woven. Hence four represents the preparation of bodily covering, the evolving of Matter from Root-Substance.

This idea is confirmed by Allendy, who says that "if the trinity, or *ternaire*, reveals to us the creative function in its essence, the number four, which follows, ought, logically, to express the result". This result, or "four-ing" process, according to Allendy, is the preparation "of the field traced out by the creative act . . . the form which is intended to enclose produced being. . . . It is, in fact, nothing else but that which we call *Nature*." He quotes also the well-known Buffon, who, in his *Vue de la Nature*, states that this prepared Sub-stance "is that part of the divine power which is manifested", which is, in other words, the "objectivity" of God. The number four is thus symbolical of the tendencies, or potentialities, of this objectivized Nature.

Numerous writers have noticed that in many languages the name of God is a word of four letters. The English word, *God*, is derived from the Persian *Goda*, Lord, and is four-lettered in several different languages : *Gott, Guth, Dieu, Alla, Deus,* and *ThEOS* (the Greek *Th* being, of course, one letter). The great God of Egypt, the supposed giver of letters to that nation, has his name spelt in various ways, as *Tehuti, Thoth, Tut,* etc., but the actual Egyptian word is *Thut*.

The four-lettered name given to God by the Hebrews is strong evidence that in ancient times they either knew these numerical doctrines or copied them from the Chaldeans and Egyptians.

This name, JHVH, may be interpreted in many ways. It may be pronounced with three breathings; or used to express the manifestation of God, literally *God's life thrown down into matter* (HVH meaning *to fall*); or used as a term signifying *he who was, is, and will be*; or, with the Yod, as representing God as the All. Apart from such orthodox and heterodox meanings, the letters themselves show that the idea of "fouring", or foundation, was expressed in the name, the foundation, that is, of all things; namely, He who produced all things and without whom nothing was made, the True Foundation.

The four letters composing the word are the Yod, the Hé, the Vauv, and the Hé, YHVH, or *Jehovah*, as it is written in English. The first letter represents manifested Power and causality; the *H* is the source of all life, the symbol of life and being, plasticity, etc.; the *Vauv* is that which unites opposites, the synthesizer, or "Holy Ghost"; whilst the final *H* shows, as a reflected image, the coming forth of life and its manifestation. The meaning of the *Four* may be materialized as Father, Mother, Holy Ghost, and Son, although the word Jehovah in Hebrew cannot be applied to the idea of the Trinity so grossly anthropomorphized and misunderstood by certain medieval and untutored Christian priests.

Now, it is obvious that the polarization of Root-Substance, unless checked, or "foured" and founded, will bring about no definite result. Polarization is merely a *beginning* of things. It is well symbolized by the cross, which shows that opposites are alone in being.

Dr. Allendy, when comparing the cross with the square, the two with the four, says that the cross, being formed on geometrical lines, does not, theoretically, occupy any surface : its arms may be prolonged indefinitely, but their only definiteness is in the central point of crossing. He therefore considers the cross a symbol of the diversity of tendencies in Nature, elementary qualities or tendencies from a certain point of view, but purely abstract. On the other hand, the square is a closed figure limiting a definite area, and inasmuch as it is equal in both dimensions, it expresses, he says, the reunion of natural tendencies, the combination of the elementary qualities. Thus the cross, according to Allendy, represents the qualities of natural things ; whereas the square represents the ideal form of materiality ; and the form, or quinaire, the matter produced. *Four* is thus the number of solidity, firmness. It is the first number, according to Philo, to show the nature of solidity.

It should be noted that it is only when referring to physical things that four is said to be the number of firmness and solidity. The idea of solidity cannot be applied to Root-Substance before it is qualified and produced, or led forth, as actual Matter. Nevertheless, the word *solidity* expresses a compression and a foundation, and in *this* sense it may be applied to cosmic beginning, for from this viewpoint *Four* represents what may be termed the concretion of the Divine Idea working in Substance. When, in any original substance, distinct qualities and opposites are produced and interact, unity manifesting as trinity, the next step will naturally be that which is typified by the number four.

For example, in the three colour primaries, red, blue, and yellow, the first interaction will produce modification, the red and yellow giving rise to green, and other interactions finally evolving the full range of seven colours. A fuller explanation of this will also be given in a later work.

This idea of foundation is shown throughout the life of Jesus, and throughout both Testaments. Jesus Himself represented the foundation of a new alignment of life, and this was obviously known to those who set down the record of His life, and did it, moreover, in such a manner as to make all the happenings therein square, or in four. Thus we have four Gospels; Jesus was Himself impaled upon the cross* and represented a figure of four—head, two outstretched arms, feet nailed together as one;† there are four guards who part His garments, each taking one part; His Name is inscribed on the cross in four letters: I.N.R.I.; the three women related to Christ who stood at the foot of the cross complete the quaternary. Other happenings in the life of Jesus emphasize the number *Four*, as at the Transfiguration, when three disciples were present with Christ; and the raising of Lazarus, who had lain four days in the tomb. All these things tend to show that the compilers of Scripture knew the full significance of this number.

The Pythagorean teaching relating to the *Four*, or Tetrad, as it was called, are not known, but hints left by those who followed the master have been

---

* Other records say "on a tree", after stoning.
† This last scene also shows the Trinity: Christ, the Great Synthesizer, between the two thieves, or Opposites.

collected by Thomas Taylor in his *Theoretic Arithmetic*, and this is, perhaps, the best work on the subject.

The Pythagoreans called the Tetrad, or *Four*, the greatest miracle, a God "after another manner than the Triad", a manifold, or rather *every*, divinity. They also considered it the fountain of natural effects and the key-bearer of Nature, and called it the "son of *Maia*", that is to say, the Son of the Mother-Substance, of the Sea of Cosmic Substance. It had, they say, the Duad for its Mother. Thus, just as the Christ may be seen as the Foundation of a new age, so four may be regarded as a symbol of the Cosmic Christ, of the result of the interaction of the cosmic Father and Mother, Life and Substance.

This idea of the Tetrad as "a God after another manner" is peculiarly interesting. God, as the Individualized Oneness, enters into relation with His Substance (Self—Not-Self), and hence, in a deep sense, is *in abscondito*, hidden, as it were, in the Opposites, in the Trinity. As the producer of worlds from that Substance which is Himself, He comes forth, figuratively, from His obscurity, and appears as His own Son. Hence, He is "God after another manner than the Triad", being Himself the producer of the manifested "gods" and all things, all processes, all "numbers".

The Pythagoreans also referred to the Tetrad as being of the nature of *Æolus*, the wind. This obviously applies to the nature of the prepared Substance, which is capable of changing, and, like the wind, "bloweth where it listeth", being alike plastic and changeful. They also called it the first

depth, as they considered the geometrical tetrad
a solid. These definitions, like the rest, show that
the number *Four* is the number of foundation,
as already said. It is, moreover, the number of
co-relation, the power without which no substance
could be prepared to ex-ist.

The word used by the Egyptians for *Four*, Aft,
means, according to its letters, *Power* (A) *going forth*
(F) *to a definite end* ('T). The idea can still be heard
in the *sound* of the modern words, as in *fier*, *vier*,
four, etc. The sound of the Greek term *Tetrad*
also conveys the idea of *a definite* (T) *rolling forth*
(R) *towards diversity* (D), and is probably derived
from the unpronounceable *Chhatri* of the Sanskrit
tongue, which has become changed to *quattuor*,
quatre, and which, later becoming *qvatre*, may have
been carelessly modified as *fier*, or *vier*, and the
English *four*, by the simple dropping of the *q*.

A consideration of the meaning of the *One*, *Two*,
and *Three* from another aspect helps considerably
to a fuller understanding of *Four*. The *One*, as
has been explained, represents *division arrested*,
and is therefore the Unity which contains all things
within itself ; the *Two* represents the first pair of
Opposites, and the *Three* that Link or Relation
between them which is sometimes called the Son,
but is more correctly termed *Fohat*, the link or
base. This is the beginning of manifestation.
But in order, as it were, to solidify or *materialize*
and co-ordinate the one, two, and three, the
"Square" has to appear, and this square is symbolized
by four.

Now, the word four in Hebrew is Arbo, or
Arbang, and contains the sign of *Potentiality*,

the *Directive* sign, and the sign of *inner development*, added to that most important symbol of materiality, the O, or Awyin. Hence the word is the emblem of multiplication, of material becoming. It may be considered as representing the "preparatory" or lesser completion which foreshadows the consummation by the seven, and is itself the prelude to that greater Completion which includes the whole of manifestation and is symbolized by the ten.

Fabre D'Olivet's description of this is interesting. It runs :

> The root of this mysterious number is RB, which, formed from the sign of directed movement and from that of generative (inner) action, includes all ideas of grandeur and multiplication. If the last character is doubled, as in RBB, this word requires an infinite numerical extension ; and if it is followed by the sign of the material sense, as in RBO, it becomes an expression of solidity, of physical (material) force, and of all ideas connected with a cube. It is in this condition that it represents the number four.*

Even considered arithmetically, four is seen to be the natural number of *foundation*, for without it no progression beyond six is possible, as is easily evident by blending the numbers one, two, and three. On the other hand, $1 + 2 = 3$, $3 + 1 = 4$, $4 + 3 = 7$, and so on, until completion is reached with the 10. In this and other ways, *Four* is shown to be the number of foundation.

Thus four is symbolic of the foundation which

---

* *La Langue Hébraïque Restituée*, v. 10 of Genesis, ch. ii.

comes after polarization, the "two-ing" process, and the synthesis, or "three-ing". Three is, practically a new unity, the One made manifest, i.e. divided into distinct, yet "affinitized", parts. These processes may be symbolized geometrically. Thus the "point" of potentiality becomes the "line" of generation, the One being made manifest as polarized opposites, two lines going off from a point, or apex, at right angles to each other. But two lines thus produced can never lead to a result. Unless there is affinity between the two as parts of a complete though polarized one-ness, there will be nothing to prevent them from rushing out indefinitely, each in its own direction. No form can be thus produced, and without form the universe could not ex-ist. Hence there is that in each which prevents complete separation, and which reunites them by the base and so forms a triangle. This triangle is the beginning of all manifestation, whether it relates to Substance or Spirit (Life), for both must be trinitized before blending can be perfectly attained.

Numbers, signs, and symbols generally, it must be remembered, are derived from Nature itself, from God, as will be clearly seen when this mystery is clearly understood. Therefore the Qabalists and Pythagoreans expressed the mysterious inner workings of Nature by means of numbers and geometrical figures; mundane arithmetic and geometry being also derived from these cosmic happenings and Ideas. Hence, in the study of these ideas and actual inner meanings of numbers, the fringe of a great mystery is touched—a mystery whose fullness can only be realized in the deepest meditation, and which will not find full expression in the dark age we live in.

Three, then, as species of a new unity, needs the powers which are within it to enlarge itself, hence three, working on itself, makes a foundation for further building, i.e. three, co-operating with one, produces four. Co-operating with two, the three produces five ; with the aid of one and two it makes six, and with the aid of four makes seven, which is the complete unfolding of Unity, as will be seen in the chapter dealing with this number.

It should be noticed, however, that the modifications of Unity and its components, one, two, and three, cannot produce more than seven by their interaction and combination. The development which is signified by the figure and number four, the triangle, $\triangle$, and its emanation, $\triangle$ is, therefore, beyond the combined work of the one, two, and three, for it leads not only to the consummation of seven, but also to the complete foundation symbolized by the ten.

If the three components are blended equally there can be no result beyond six, but if one of them predominates over the rest, as 3 + 1, 3 + 2, etc., then the numbers four to seven are generated. A "seven-ing" thus represents a cycle of accomplishment, a "rest", or "Sabbathizing", after creation, not, of course, a *rest* in the physical sense, as is ordinarily understood from the words of the Book of Genesis, for God, who is Absolute Motion itself, is necessarily beyond the opposites known to man as *activity* and *rest*.

Thus this new manifestation of the Trinity, the four, or Son, has to be reflected, i.e. added to itself, or, rather, to its component parts, three plus one, to produce eight. Five, six, and seven, as seen above, have already been produced by the interaction of the four with the three principles, one, two, and three. Again, four working with the three and two gives rise to nine, and completion comes when four is added to all the numbers produced, as $4 + 3 + 2 + 1 = $ ten. This is the end of simple numeration and becoming, and after it, both cosmically and arithmetically, all is repetition and multiplication.

Now, if a cycle of evolution, or of ideas, be considered as having seven stages, the lowest stage of descent will always be the fourth. Hence four is, for this reason also, considered as the number of depth or foundation, as base, the lowest stage, and yet the foundation or stage leading to the highest.

The ancients, who understood the qualities contained in the number, built their ideas accordingly, and a full description of the many different quaternaries which have accordingly arisen is given by Agrippa, and also, but more completely, by Allendy. The Hebrews, as we have seen, used four as the number of foundation, their name for God being itself four-lettered and conveying this idea. The Christian conception of Father, Mother, Holy Ghost, and Son, is also four-square. Other quaternaries are the four Great Angels who preside over the quarters of the Universe, the four Great Beings who rule the elements, the four Beings, the Lion, the Eagle, the Ox, and the Man, the four Gospels, the four Seasons, the four fundamental states of Matter, and many others.

CHAPTER VIII

FIVE, according to its root meaning, is the number of harvesting, of arranging the "sheaves" of the produced Substance, the hitherto potential substance which now becomes matter, i.e. becomes manifest, and from its combinations produces all the different grades of matter, as known—a process especially fascinating in its outworking to those who know the meaning of cosmic numbering and the arithmetical, progressive phases of the creation and evolution of a universe.

As the earthly harvest is gathered in by the farmer, and arranged to suit his need and requirement, so, in a deeper sense, God, the Harvester, having produced Substance and prepared it for the foundation of worlds, now gathers it to Himself, the *Four* to the *One*, to qualify it, to prepare it for use and nourishment, to build up forms and worlds therefrom.

After the correlation of the primordial Substance, and the foundation by the "four-ing" process, or Son, the Logos or manifestation, the "Word" or Vibratory Power of God in Nature, "broods over the waters of the deep", over the ocean of plastic stuff in Space. This brooding, as the Scriptures term it, is the action of God's "Mind" (if such a term is permissible), preparing from the manifested matter (4), grade upon grade, element upon element, of matter, qualifications from within the previously potential, affinitized, stabilized Substance.

The "Mind" of God brooding over this plastic medium, this manifested matter, produces from it exteriorized qualities which till then were mere possibilities locked up within it—locked up, as it were, in the depths of God and His Substance. These qualities, *sub*sisting in Matter, need the action of God's "Mind", the "five-ing" or harvesting process, to produce them and bring them to *existence*.

Five thus represents a kind of spreading-out process, and may be symbolized by the geometrical form, the pentagon, with its five points, which is also the symbol of a perfect humanity. This spreading-out process produces from the prepared Substance the modifications called qualities. Hence five is the symbol of matter produced for purposes of creation.

If these ideas as to the qualifying of matter are not familiar to the reader, he may find additional help towards their understanding in Chapters I and II. It should clearly be realized that if matter is to be useful for creative purposes, it *must* be polarized, just as the original Life-Substance was polarized. Thus, through this "five-ing" process, there arises a trinity of matter, as before there was a trinity of Life or Spirit, and by this new trinity the Root-Matter is spread out and made definitely manifest ; and therefore it is said in *The Secret Doctrine*,* "Five represents the universal quintessence

---

* *Ibid.*, vol. ii, p. 617.

which spreads in every direction and forms all matter."*

Dr. Allendy says that five is the symbol of all forms of matter, and refers especially to the physical plane. He also quotes a writer who states that this number of matter possesses five properties, viz. form, divisibility, impenetrability, dissolubility, and inertia. Again, it is said that five forms are combined in the different chemical atoms, all of which, the tetrahedron, the cube, the octohedron, the dodecahedron, and the isosahedron, have equal angles, sides, and superficies, and are known as Pythagorean forms. They are found manifesting in all crystals.†

Allendy, who further explains the different properties of manifestation, says that the number five is the symbol of material existence, or the objectivity of things, Life in its different degrees. This, however, obviously refers to Matter rather than to Life, especially as he considers it necessary to conceive life in the sense of its extension as a cosmic principle; yet he separates the ideas of Life and Matter, and shows that number represents the relation between these two. The number five expresses, according to this writer, not a state, but an act. It is a passage, a transition. Matter is not, as philosophers have known from the earliest times, a for-ever fixed and determined condition, but a transitory arrangement of atomized stuff always

---

* This is a quotation from a manuscript by the Freemason Ragon, who declares it to be the work of M. le Comte de St. Germain, the distinguished, though unofficial, ambassador between many European Courts during the French Revolution.

† See especially *Occult Chemistry*, by Annie Besant and C. W. Leadbeater, a remarkable book.

possible of resolution into its primordial un-conditionedness.

Whereas, then, four may be considered as the number of formation and foundation, or conception, five would be the number of birth, of actual material commencement. As has been said, and is here taken for granted, there is no life without form, and no form which does not contain life. But that Matter should be so ensouled is not sufficient ; it is necessary also that both Matter and Life should be "qualified", should have qualities, that gradation and diversity may alike result.

Without this qualifying, this "five-ing" process, or harvesting, Matter, as we know it, could never have existed ; and thus five, as Allendy well says, is the symbol of the creative Power of God, manifested as the "Word" or Logos, the Trinity, showing itself forth through the Binary ; for these two, the three and the two, are five, cosmically and arithmetically. In other words, the Infinite expresses Itself in the finite, the one added to, and co-operating with, the four, produces five, Nature itself. It is interesting in this connection to recall that *Pente*, the Greek five, is derived from Pan, which represents Nature, the All, and was sacred to Juno, the goddess representing receptivity, or Substance.

The Hebrew word for five, *Chumisch*, is also extremely helpful in understanding Cosmic becoming. D'Olivet defines it as referring to "facultative comprehension", that is to say, the faculty for comprehending a collectivity of things with ease and convenience, a gathering-in, or arranging. Chapter V of Genesis, it will be noted, contains a description of all the emanated beings, and is devoted solely to generation ; hence D'Olivet calls it the chapter of facultative comprehension. He evidently does not read it as a history of the generation of all the beings who followed Adam, but as a description of generation in a cosmic sense.

Five, in Hebrew, is also said by D'Olivet to express a movement of contraction and apprehension such as would result from the grasping of a thing, the whole hand, the five fingers, pressing tightly and warming it. The root of the word, he says, is dual, the first root, ChM, pointing out the effect of the second, MSh ; that is to say, the former depicts the general envelopment, the heat which results, and the effect of the contractive movement caused by the latter.

Thus the root, ChM, has the symbol of effort, Ch, joined to the letter M, which, as the reader knows, represents the mass, or aggregation, of Substance ; that from which all is extracted, the letter being used, even grammatically, to express the idea of *from*. This root means, literally, *warmth*, that which results from contraction. On the other hand, MSh represents a movement *of a mass* towards contraction, and hence gives rise to *mass, mess, mush*, etc., as is shown by the word *Moses*, which means *he who was extracted* (M) *from the plastic Substance* (MSh), or, literally, *he who was drawn out of the water*. Hence, MSh, meaning *the mass* and *a movement*, blended with ChM, *warmth*, show that this word, the Hebrew *Five*, represents a collecting together, or harvesting, and an arranging by contraction of the prepared parts of matter. The root MSh also signifies *that which is compact*, a crop or harvest, anything which is extracted, or drawn out from, an already existing matter, as is shown by its letters individually.

It is obvious that the meaning of the Hebrew word for *Five* is the same as that already expressed in these pages, and, when referred to cosmic happenings, relates to the stirring up of the prepared matter, the arranging of it into "sheaves", as for a harvest. In other words, it refers to the *qualification* of matter by the "Mind" of God, and the production of a base from which the requisite grades of matter should result. This harvesting, or maturing, of the differentiated matter is the half-way stage of the cosmic processes, and the result is the definite building up of the atoms, molecules, and elements from which globes or worlds will ultimately result.

Even arithmetically, five is seen to be the centre of all simple numbers, as the reader will find by studying the numbers 1, 2, 3, 4, 5, 6, 7, 8, and 9. If these are arranged as squares, either as

$$
\begin{array}{ccc}
1 & 2 & 3 \\
4 & 5 & 6 \\
7 & 8 & 9
\end{array}
$$

or

$$
\begin{array}{ccc}
1 & 4 & 7 \\
2 & 5 & 8 \\
3 & 6 & 9
\end{array}
$$

the five is always at the centre. Evidently it was for these reasons that the Pythagoreans named it *cardiatis*, or *cordialis*, the heart of things manifested, the centre of all things and numbers, the heart being the centre of the body.*

The number was called many strange names by Pythagorean writers. It was *the privation of strife, the unconquered, change of quality, light and justice, the Tower of Jupiter, a stable axis,* etc. These definitions have caused "the enemy to blaspheme", and to declare that the Pythagorean doctrines with regard to numbers are nonsensical; but the terms are quite clear to those who have the key. Thus *change of quality* is stated by an anonymous Pythagorean writer † to represent the Five, that which "changes all things triply extended or which have length, breadth, and depth into the sameness of a sphere and producing light". Taylor confirms this by saying that Five is eminently a circular number, and spherical, terminating itself, or restoring itself, in every multiplication.

This idea of change of quality, as applied to the birth of a universe, confirms all that is set down here by the present writer, and is undoubtedly correct, the "five-ing" period being that of the arranging and harvesting of the growth, the gathering of the result of growth in the cosmic field, and the qualifying and grading the produce according to quality. Unless such a change occurs, there can be no adequate distribution of matter, and no manifestation.

The term *privation of strife* shows that the opposition which was necessary to produce the matter required for the building of the universe has, in a sense, now ceased, that all things which

---

* *Theoretic Arithmetic,* by Thomas Taylor, p. 194.
† Quoted by Taylor, p. 192.

were founded (4) and separated out are now constituted and re-integrated for the new stage of
change of quality.

The number was apparently called *a stable axis*
because it stirs up matter whilst itself remaining
firm and definite and, as a power of God, brooding,
selecting, re-arranging, planning-out, and drawing
out the qualities required, sorting out, as it were,
the different grades within the prepared Substance,
changing their condition from latency to patency.
It is also well called *the privation of strife*, for when
the "five-ing" process is completed, all things,
spirit and matter, life and form, have become
harmoniously blended, linked together, in sympathy.

The anonymous writer quoted by Taylor says
further that the *Pentad*, the five, was called *Nemesis*
because it "distributes in an appropriate manner
things celestial and divine"—which, again, is
confirmatory of all that has been said in these
pages.

According to Agrippa, the number five has a
great power, composed as it is of numbers representing male and female. It is, moreover, the exact
half of the universal number, or number of completion, the Ten, and it is consequently called the
number of marriage. It was dedicated to Mercury,
the God of Mind, which is the link between Spirit
and Matter, and this was but natural, since *Five*
represents the effect of the Mind, or spirit, of God
which after the Foundation (4) came forth to brood
over and prepare the "waters of space", i.e. to
"create" from the base it had produced in the
"fouring" process.

The Hebrew names of God all show a progression

in number. Thus the triple name is ShDI, the quaternary is YHVH, Jehovah. In later years the Rosicrucians introduced *Sh* into the middle of the word Jehovah, and some people imagine it to have been done in order to make the word represent *Jesus*; but it was merely a "blind", the name being in reality a symbol of God as Saviour. It was written YHShUH, and pronounced *yehushiah*, and was sometimes called the *Ineffable Pentagram.* Other Hebrew words are used in this manner, as, for example, the Three Yods, denoting *God as Abstract Trinitizing Power*; the four-lettered ADNI, or *Lord God*, and the well-known ALH, *God*, and ALHIM, *God as Collectivity of Power*. All these names of God show in a peculiarly illuminating manner the cosmic unfolding by rhythmic progression.

CHAPTER IX

THE number five, as we have seen, represents that
Cosmic process during which Matter is qualified,
separated into kinds, and arranged, like the harvest,
for *use*. By this action of God's "Mind", three
fundamental qualities, or, as it were, three colours
or tones, are produced from and within the prepared
matter ; and as there are three qualities of matter,
so there are also three aspects of God or Spirit,
and these now find their reflection in the more
material trinity.

God, or Life, is triple, and has three aspects :
the Will to create, the Wisdom or Love which
contrives and holds together the creation, and the
Creative Activity or Mind which sends forth and
causes the appearance of that which is created.
These Three, known by many and various names
in the different religions of the world, are, however,
considered metaphysically rather than physically in
these pages.

The number six represents that period in the
creative processes in which Matter is prepared as
a triplicity, and Spirit, already a triplicity, ensouls
it. This separation of the one-ness of matter into
manyness results, under the action of the triple
aspects of the one Life, in the production of three
main modes of motion in matter, i.e. three types

of matter having fundamentally different modes of motion. The appearance or manifestation of these two trinities of Spirit and Matter, which, it should be remembered, are but polarized or manifested unities, is the "six-ing" process, six—twice three— representing that which relates the opposites, links triangle to triangle, trinity of Spirit to trinity of Matter.

The double triangle is a symbol of this process of inter-relation. Polarized Life becomes blended with polarized Matter; harmonized, and definitely linked together, they form a combination from which alone true creation, i.e. the definite building-up of bodies, can result. Hence six is the number of balance, harmony, junction, and proportion; and as the double of three it reflects the ideas represented by that number. Its symbol is the so-called Solomon's Seal, the interlaced triangles, the symbol, as is well known, of the junction of Spirit and Matter, Life and Form.

The Pythagorean idea that six is the symbol of the soul is interesting, and not difficult of understanding in the light of the above. As Matter and Spirit are thus linked, life everywhere ensouls Matter, a balance is attained between them, and all is ready for actual creation, the Soul of the Universe having thus become mingled with all things. And since it is in much the same manner that the soul is linked to the body, *Six* may quite truly be said to be a symbol of the soul; indeed, many schools of thought teach that man is a septenary being, the seventh principle being the Self within the forms, the Atma, the point in the "double triangle" whereby Spirit and Matter are blended and synthesized. This view represents the "Point" as the Reality behind all things, and shows Spirit linked to body by means of soul, which thus becomes the link between man and his higher Self.

It should not be difficult to understand why the Greek philosophers called this number, or process, *harmony, the perfection of parts, nuptial, Venus, peace, friendship, health,* and *truth,* for all these descriptions signify *a coming together, a junction, a wholeness* (health), in short, a synthesizing process.

Six was also called *the distinct union of the parts* of the universe, because soul is, as it were, "the animated form of formless matter",* and was termed *gamos, a marriage,* and *gamelia, nuptials,* which again convey the idea of junction, or union.

The remarks of Thomas Taylor in his *Theoretic Arithmetic* as to the reason for the epithet *truth* as applied to this number are very enlightening, especially to those who understand the stage in the Cosmic process of becoming which the number *Six* represents. "It was, perhaps, so called", he says, "because truth is the *harmonic conjunction of that which is known with that which knows.*" The words italicized convey precisely the same meaning as that expressed in this work.

The harmony and blending represented by the number *Six* is a blending of opposites, and a harmony of complementaries. Dr. Allendy evidently holds the same idea, for he states in his *Le Symbolisme des Nombres* that "with the number six is inaugurated the second half of the series of simple numbers.

---

* *Animated modes* in matter would be a better expression than *animated form.*

In virtue of the idea which is attached to the Binary, the two, the two halves of the series ought to present, the one by its relation to the other, an opposition in a general sense. If we consider, in its ensemble, the first half . . . we see in it the progressive transformation from the Absolute to the world of matter and being, it assists us to understand the ideal steps of creation. The incognizable Cause (Unity) becomes successively the principle of differentiation (Binary), of the action of organization (Ternary), of realized or founded form (Quaternary). This is, in a sense, a kind of degradation of the Absolute, Its dispersion in a multiplicity of creatures, Its descent into matter. By opposition, the second half of the series 1-10 ought to point out the way of return", that is, the way of return to complete unity, as symbolized by the 10, the perfect number, the way towards reintegration, as shown by the numbers 7, 8, 9, and 10.

Allendy further shows that the number six is a paired or even number, and that it ought, as such, to signify a principle of equilibrium, "a static correspondence between two analogous terms and not a transitory action or passage from one state to another. It is the instrument of progression, but not the progression itself." This is, of course, correct, for it is the number seven which represents this progression, i.e. the atomization of matter without which all building would be impossible.*

All that has been said herein with regard to the trinities of Spirit and Matter is confirmed by Dr. Allendy, though of necessity in different words. He states that the study of the number six

---

* See under Chapter X, *The Number Seven.*

as a double trinity is interesting, as showing the
state of equilibrium which results from the
opposition of the two trinitized organizations, of
two actions—the first represented as 1, 2, 3, the
Logos and His phases of creative organization ;
and the second, which is opposed to it, or set in
opposition to it, being its reflection in the world
of forms (creatures). Thus, four is the body of
Nature, five represents the productions which
replenish it, whilst six is the action, or interaction,
of the created powers. "The six thus represents
the opposition of the creature (matter) to the
Creator (Spirit) in an indefinite equilibrium."
This is the essential nature of the number six.

That this number should be called justice by the
Greeks seems curious until the idea of a balancing
up of all things is remembered. That there is a
Justice ruling all things and persons in the universe,
a "Law which moves to righteousness, which none
at last can turn aside or stay", as Sir Edwin Arnold
puts it in his *Light of Asia*, is an immemorable belief.
The Hindus and Buddhists call it the Law of
Karma, or Cause and Effect ; the Christian sums
it up in the belief "as a man sows, so shall he reap",
and the Hebrew by the term *Mischpotim*, literally
Judgments. It is this Law, the intimate relation
of Cause and Effect, Action and Reaction, Force
and Form, which is symbolized by the *Six*, the
number of balance.

This number may also be said to represent the
fullness of all things, the extent of materiality, and,
in a sense, Space. Some thinkers consider that there
are but six extensions or directions : up and down,
left and right, before and behind. The relation of

Soul to body is also seen as a senary, as by the Alchemists, who expressed it in the terms Sulphur, Salt, and Mercury, which, with their polarizations, make six in all. The Hindu philosophers speak of three modes or qualities of matter, viz. *Sattva*, *Rajas*, and *Tamas*, in which work the three modes of motion ; these fill the manifested universe, containing all things and entering into the make-up of all things, no further qualification being possible, all other modifications of the universe being seen as the result of the interaction of these opposites, trinitized matter and trinitized force. The same idea may be traced in Colour and Music. All such senaries, or sixes, have, however, a point of meeting, a point which unites them, and this point is the seven, the fundamental number, the number of numbers, the accomplishment of all things, as will later be seen.

According to the orthodox interpretation of Genesis, the world was created in six days; better terms, however, would be six periods, or progressions. In any case, it represents the fullness of creation, as is shown by the "resting" of God on the seventh "day". In this creation of a Universe, the One as Spirit and the One as Matter become trinitized, and these two trinities open the way for the "seven-ing" process. This "seven-ing" process has, however, no relation to "rest" ; it shows only *accomplishment*.

This word "accomplishment" conveys practically the same idea and is a far better explanation, for God, being Eternal Motion itself, cannot be said to "rest". It should be noted, however, that the Book of Genesis bears little relation to the creation of our own globe, except in a very reflected sense, analogically. It is primarily a history of, or a formula of the creation of the whole Universe in Space, as will be explained in a later work, *The Book of Genesis Unveiled (II)*. Meanwhile students may find it interesting to note that each one of the first ten chapters of Genesis represents one epoch in the cosmic process of becoming. Each chapter, of the first ten, will be found to represent one of these creative epochs, or stages, and in fact the number of the chapter is as much a key to its meaning as is the matter treated therein.

Fabre D'Olivet has pointed out in his *La Langue Hébraïque Restituée* that the ideas in Chapter I of Genesis may be summed up under the heading *Principiation*; those in Chapter II by *Distinction*; those in Chapter III by *Extraction*; those in Chapter IV by *Divisional Multiplication*; and those in Chapter V by *Facultative Comprehension*. Chapter VI shows by its contents the idea of a balancing of things for further development (*the Flood*); and this chapter is described by D'Olivet as *Proportional Measurement*. The remaining chapters are dealt with in the same way.

As is well known to all Qabalistic students, the commentaries on Genesis make, as related in the *Sepher Ha-Zohar*, a play on the first word of Genesis, whereby the word BRAShITh is made to read as BRA, *he has created*, and ShITh six,* instead of as a complete word, BRAShITh, *in the beginning*, or *in Principle*, in the sense of commencement. This is, of course, only a play

---

* The Hebrew word for "six" is ShSh, or *Shishi*; the Chaldaic, ShTh, *Shisi*.

upon words, but it may be understood from it that God created by means of "six-ing", that is, by bringing together and balancing the two opposite trinities of Force and Matter. Indeed, this idea is the exact inner meaning of the name of the letter *Vauv*, which is used as the numeral six in Hebrew, and is pictured as a link, a hook, and is a symbol of that which unites in order to change from one state to another. Hence, probably, the inventors of the Tarot cards have made the sixth card represent Love, the great unifier.

Fabre D'Olivet, apparently the only writer who has properly translated the words used by the Hebrews to describe numbers, says that the root of the Hebrew word for six is ShU, which represents all ideas of *equality*, of *readiness*, of *equilibrium*. When this root is added to the symbol Sh, which represents motion, or, as D'Olivet calls it, relative duration, the result, ShSh, or Shishi, becomes, he says, "the symbol of every proportional measure". The same writer further states that it is well known that the number six is applied to the measure of the circle in particular, and in general to all proportional measures.

Now, six in Hebrew is somewhat difficult of description, for it contains but one letter twice repeated, viz. ShSh—that is to say, the sign of relative duration, or circumscribed motion, doubled. This shows its relation to three, which also contains the sign in double. Thus six, ShSh, is a densification of three, ShLUSh, minus the two signs L and U; it is, in fact, a densification of the three Idea (which, as we have seen, is itself a kind of Unity, containing Three in One), and its reflection on a lower plane, showing that equilibrium has been attained. Here again is a suggestion of the above and the below, the two triangles interlaced, Spirit and Matter blended.

When this stage arrives, the Consummation is at hand, the "seven-ing", whether creative (beginning) or destructive (ending), as in the case of the Flood of the seventh chapter of Genesis. As Three is a completion, or unity in trinity, of Spirit, so Six is a completion, a unity in trinity, of Matter ; and the link between,* the synthesizing Point, makes Seven, the Consummation.

---

* The *Fohat* of the Buddhist.

CHAPTER X

ACCORDING to Dr. Allendy, the number seven has very great relation with the number three, for in virtue of its double reflection it is to the ternary what the ternary is to Unity. Since three represents the development of a principle, the seven ought to represent the principle doubly developed, that is to say, manifested and objectively realized. Allendy mentions, in this connection, the three fundamental colours, red, yellow, and blue, which, in their combinations, give rise to all shades.

With their intermediaries, these principles follow a natural serial development in the spectrum, and give rise to seven definite divisions : (1), the primary red ; (2), orange, the intermediary between red and yellow ; (3), yellow itself, as a primary colour ; (4), green, the stage between yellow and blue ; (5), primary blue. Between red and blue there are two shades instead of one : (6), indigo, which is a densified blue, and (7), violet, the true intermediary. He also notes the seven stages in Music ; these, like the colours of the spectrum, are not in any way arbitrarily divided, but respond to the sounds of Nature and to the natural function of the human voice. The seven notes may be considered as proceeding from a fundamental Trinity of which the parts are in perfect accord,

ut—mi—sol being produced by means of intermediaries, and by a doubling of *sol* in *la* (as indigo is a
doubling of blue). He says also that if the limitation
of perceptible sounds is extended to ten octaves,
the musical cycle is composed of seven.

Allendy further points out that the number four
is the measure of phenomena which present themselves without cessation during a series, whilst
seven is a measure of evolutionary cycles of which
the succession in Music gives a very exact idea of a
spiral progression which never returns to its original
state. This spiral evolution is, as he says, a very
good symbol of the "seven-ing" process; seven
representing not a closed and completed circle,
but a cycle, or spiral, preparatory to the completion
of a process.*

The same writer records an interesting fact in
connection with the six-pointed star on a central
point. He says that the Point, the seven, is the
open door between Heaven and Earth, and that
this is the reason why the rainbow and its seven
colours, which was supposed to have appeared after
the deluge, was considered as a sign of the alliance
between Earth and Heaven. Seven, he suggests,
is a bridge between the Three Persons of the
Trinity and the three natural principles; for whilst
six expresses merely a static equilibrium, the
reflection of the Creator in Form (*la créature*),
seven shows the Creator directing matters by means
of a graded and spiral evolution.†

All this is in perfect accord with what has
already been written in this work, and should be
compared with what is said here regarding the

---

* *Le Symbolisme des Nombres*, p. 172.   † *Ibid.*, p. 178.

"seven-ing" process in which the atomization of matter proceeds. This process is, as already shown, by no means a static equilibrium, as in the six stage, but a violent reaction, a definite, directive commencement of actual material evolution.

Allendy quotes further the many passages from the Bible which show that the number seven was considered in a special sense, and connected with all holy matters. The reader might trace this for himself in the Scriptures ; for though the study of such passages does not explain the meaning of the number, the manner in which it was used by the Hebrews show that they understood its inner significance. He adds that the Hebrews used the word "seven" in the sense of taking an oath, and offers a very questionable proof of this from Genesis xxi, 30 ; but of this an explanation will be given later.

Whilst the number six represents harmonious conjunction, the linking up of Spirit and Matter, of Life and Form, nevertheless, in this stage, there are only qualities or kinds of matter, and modes of motion, or Spirit, working within it. These opposites, like those of the primordial Trinity— Three—produce nothing if left to themselves. Thus the "seven-ing" process is as necessary to the polarized and opposite trinities, the blended six, as the "four-ing" process was necessary to the Trinity. In other words, Matter must be atomized or no building up of forms and bodies can result, for unless this atomization takes place all remains in a state of flux. Each particle of Matter has, therefore, to be individualized, and this necessitates the production of primordial and ultimate atoms.

Matter, having been prepared by the "five-ing"

process, and the balance struck between the opposites in the "six-ing" stage, is now ready for perfect production, for definite formation. With the disturbing of the balance, a new stage commences, and this new stage is the "seven-ing" process, the process of atomization. This disturbing of the balance causes a "terrible catastrophe", as symbolized in Chapter VII of Genesis, which tells of the Flood, the waters that "covered the earth". In like manner, the sudden changing of Matter into separate, distinct, and independent particles naturally causes these, by reason of the energizing life within them, to rush away from the previous state of balance or unification in the mass, and become strangers to each other ; and this is the first stage of Division.

An illustration of this on a small scale is seen when a body "dies". With the withdrawal of the spirit, there is no power left for holding the unity, the body, together ; and the myriads upon myriads of atoms, molecules, etc., which constituted a unity as long as the dynamic energy of the spirit remained as a central Force holding them in check, now endeavour to rush away from the unity which formerly contained them, producing, in the act, heat, friction, vibrations of a peculiar kind, and odours not sympathetically contacted by a refined nature. From what happens in this case, we may understand dimly what happens when the balance between the polarized trinities of spirit and matter is broken, and the resulting atomized particles spread out everywhere—a veritable "flood" of matter in Space.

As said before, the first ten chapters of the Book of Genesis show analogically, by their happenings, what happens at creation, each chapter showing forth one stage of the Cosmic processes. Thus in the sixth chapter a preparation is made for the catastrophe to come in the seventh, viz. the Flood. Fabre D'Olivet, describing the happenings recorded in the seventh chapter, says that this "seventh chapter represents consummation; the equilibrium is broken, a terrible catastrophe follows, and the Universe is renewed". He does not say clearly that this represents a flood of cosmic matter in Space rather than an earthly engulfment; but it should be noted that he says it was the "Universe" which was renewed, and not the earth. However, there is little doubt that this chapter and its number, seven, together represent the idea of a breaking-up of a mass, or unity, the resulting tumescence, and the renewal of things which follows it.

The first effect of this disturbance is the apparent disintegration of all matter : the separated atoms rush out to enjoy their liberty, but as the Law of Affinity is working through all, each atom immediately commences to look for its complement, the fact being that atoms are differently polarized, some being positive, some negative, some "male" and some "female", and others neutral.

Now, the ordinary scientist posits the atom as the smallest indivisible portion of matter, and, though unable to see it, proves its existence by many experiments. There are, however, scientists of a different school who have seen and thoroughly examined the atom, and have given their report on it in such detail, and in such a reasonable and logical manner, that no unbiased or scientific mind could possibly dispute their findings, although it might dispute their claim of examining the atom at first hand. The work in which these investigations are recorded, *Occult Chemistry*, is the first contribution to what will one day be a great Science, the Science of the (at present) unseen. Modern scientists who read this epoch-making work will assuredly find that it reveals to them the meaning of matters on which they have hitherto pondered unsuccessfully, and will help them to put the knowledge received to practical, scientific use.

Occult Chemistry shows that the primordial atom is formed by force flowing into a certain space and pressing back the undifferentiated stuff, the finest rudiment of matter, which is everywhere in the universe and which forms the oval or circular "wall" of the atom.* It is this atomization of matter which constitutes the "seven-ing" process.

Seven, as has already been said, is the fullness of the unfolding power of manifested unity, showing itself forth as a trinity of powers, or qualities, the blending or interaction of which can produce no more than seven states, or kinds. This is clearly seen in Colour : from the "white" light, which is not a colour, but is the *essence* of colour, come forth the three primaries, and from the blending of these three others are produced, the seventh being the first step towards a return to nothingness or non-manifestation. There are thus only seven definite colours from the one, tertiaries being grades which tend towards the negation of colour, the densest shade of which is black, absolute negation. (There are, of course, many *shades* of colour, just as there

---

* A further description of the atom, its ways and make-up, will be found in the work in question.

are many degrees of matter, but it should be understood that there are only three fundamental grades, and that the seven unfold from this trinity in unity.)

It is curious to note in this connection that the name given to the number seven by the Greeks was, amongst many others, Minerva, the goddess said to have been born from the head of Jupiter, the first of the gods, the One. Taylor, commenting on this, says that as Minerva proceeded from the head of Jupiter, "so the heptad proceeds from the monad which is the head or summit of number".* This shows, as is suggested in this work, that the number seven represents a consummation of things, i.e. the completion of any cycle whatever, and its returning upon itself.

That seven is the number which symbolizes Unity unfolded to its limit and ready for appearance and manifestation can be seen also by a study of physiological science and genetics. The human fœtus, as is well known, quickens, as a general rule, at the seventh month, and is actually ready for birth as a completed body, although it is not normally born until the end of the ninth (lunar) month. The number nine, it will be shown, is the number of a change of condition, whilst the ten represents the coming forth as a completion. Thus the child is actually born under the number ten, the sign of completion, although seven is the period of consummation or cyclic completion, the period when the fœtus is a living, pulsating, and completed being.

It is generally accepted that the human body develops in stages of seven, and renews itself in these cycles of growth, becoming eventually outworn at

---

* *Theoretic Arithmetic*, p. 200.

the completion of the ninth cycle of "seven-ing". This is, of course, only a general rule. The tenth septenary (ten being the number of completion) usually marks the end of life, the days of a man being "threescore years and ten and even by reason of strength fourscore years". Seven may be seen as the number of all creative acts, the consummation or cyclic completion, examples of which are too well known and too numerous to be considered here.

The remaining stages after this completion simply represent the arrangement and maturing of the created forms, and the coming forth into life and existence, the perfecting of things, the completion which contains the cyclic completion or consummation. Thus in the unfolding of numbers may be traced the history of any creation, whether of a whole universe, a world, or the human fœtus. They are the symbols which demonstrate the history of creation.

Cornelius Agrippa states that seven is a number of varied and multiple power, being composed of 1 + 6, 2 + 5, or 3 + 4, and having the Unity to balance the double trinity. Hence, as already said, the double triangle with the synthesizing point within it, the so-called Solomon's Seal, or Shield of David, is a true symbol of this Natural Rhythm, or number.

"The virtue of this number", says Agrippa, "serves also for the generation of man, conception, birth and nourishment and development." He shows that all these things are developed on septenary lines, and points out that the Pythagoreans call this number the number of virginity, because it is the first, which can no longer be engendered, and which does not itself generate; that is to say, it is the extreme unfoldment of unity after polarization. "It cannot be divided into two equal parts," says Agrippa, "inasmuch as it is not built up from two equal numbers." He also records that it was sacred to Pallas, and that it was used by the Hebrews in the sense of taking an oath, but he does not explain how the number seven could have so been used. This explanation will, however, be forthcoming in its own place.

Medical evidence is not wanting to show that this "seven-ing" period is found in all manifested things. Thus we read in the *Medical Review*:

> There is a harmony of numbers in all nature : in the force of gravity, in the planetary movements, in the laws of heat, light and electricity, and chemical affinity, in the forms of animals and plants, in the perceptions of the mind. The direction, indeed, of modern natural and physical science is towards a generalization which shall express the fundamental laws of all, by one simple numerical ratio. We would refer to Professor Whewell's *Philosophy of the Inductive Science*, and to Mr. Hay's researches into the laws of harmonious colouring and form. From these it appears that the number seven is distinguished in the laws regulating the harmonious perception of forms, colours, and sounds, and probably of taste also, if we could analyse our sensations of this kind with mathematical accuracy.*

The idea that the "seven-ing" process in the Universe is that of atomization seems to be confirmed by Oswald Wirth in his *Le Livre Du Compagnon*, the Book of the Fellow-Craft, or Craftsman, of Freemasonry. "Seven", he says, "is the number

---

* The *Medical Review*, July 1846.

of the harmony which results after a just arrangement between dissimilar elements." And it is curious that one may describe the atomization of matter, in one sense, as a disturbance, and in another as harmony resulting from such an arrangement, but such is, of course, the case, paradoxical as it seems at first sight. Seven is thus the number of harmony, inasmuch as it symbolizes the completed process of polarization, as is evident from a study of the double triangle with the central point which represents the synthesis of all things.

It is interesting to note that during the six "days" of creation of the Book of Genesis, only Elohim (God) is mentioned, whereas after the creation of man, on the sixth day, the work is carried on by Jehovah-Elohim. Jehovah thus represents God as the Life outpoured for the benefit of man and creation generally ; and means, amongst other things, the life of God thrown down into, or immanent in, all things. It should be noted also that the creation of man, which has been described in Chapter I as the work of the Elohim (God), is referred to in Chapter II as the work of Jehovah-Elohim (Lord-God) ; and that whilst the Elohim created man "in his own image", the Lord-God breathes into his nostrils the breath of life, to make him a "living soul".

This confirms the idea that Jehovah represents the Life which does not function until Matter is ready ; this occurs only on the "seventh day", the day on which God is said to "rest". The seventh stage of creation is thus not entirely a new departure, but a stage or condition in which all the previous work is summed up. Hence it is only on the seventh day and after that Jehovah and Elohim appear as one, and Life works through Creation, or, in another sense, to be explained more fully in a later work, that the Creative Powers work in conjunction with God's descending life.

The idea that seven is the consummation of all the stages summed up in six is illustrated in the well-known jewel of Freemasonry, the Cube, which is made to open, and unfolds as a cross of four perpendicular and three horizontal squares. This shows that the six, as the cube, when unfolded or spread out, itself produces the seven. As in the double triangle there is the point or Power which is common to both, so in the unfolded cube there is the point, or central square, belonging equally to both arms of the cross.

Railston Skinner, in his brilliant *Source of Measures*, draws attention to this in a noticeable manner, although he makes no attempt to explain its significance.

"It is very observable", he says, "that while there are but six faces to a cube, the representation of the cross as the cube unfolded, as to the cross-bars, displays one face of the cube as common to two bars and counted as belonging to either; then while the faces originally represented are but six, the use of the two bars counts the squares as four for the upright and three for the crossbar, making seven in all. Here we have the famous 4 and 3 and 7." *

Seven is written in Hebrew, ShVO, and pronounced Shveer, or Shve-o; and our English word *swear*, through the German *schwerin*, is, according

---

* *Ibid.,* p. 50.

to Fabre D'Olivet, derived from it. He says that in Hebrew to take a Shveer, to affirm upon the sacred seven, means to take an oath that a certain thing shall be accomplished,* the fundamental meanings of seven and *swear* being identical.

The root of the word, ShUV or ShV, expresses, according to the best authorities, the idea of return. It is sometimes used to denote old age (second childhood, which is a return), and also the completion of a cycle, a consummation, or, as D'Olivet puts it, "a return to the place from which one set out". This root is joined to the root OU meaning a cycle, or "to turn upside down" (Parkhurst), hence a revolution. Thus the word "seven" means not only one thing repeated seven times, but refers also to a cycle of days, weeks, or ages, during which a certain work—human, terrestrial, or cosmic—is consummated, and returns on a higher spiral, with the additional characteristics moulded into it during the "sevening" period, to the *status quo ante*. After these periods of "sevening", whether weeks, ages, or periods of evolution, man and the Universe return to rest to prepare for a new revolution or "sevening": this is the ShBTh, the Sabbath,† or day of consummation.

From this the teachings regarding the "sevening" potentiality of man may be understood. He comes down the ladder of evolution with all his powers *latent*, returning gradually, step by step, until the cycle is completed, and all his powers have become *patent*. Now a Master, he takes his place at the head

---

* Parkhurst says the same.
† Sabbath is not a holy day, but *literally* a Sevening day (consummation).

of his lodge, employing and instructing his brethren in all the arts and crafts. He is now a perfect focus for the rays of Intuition, the Spiritual Sun, and capable of giving light to toiling pilgrims who, but for him, would tread the path in darkness.

The meanings of three, five, and seven show clearly the instructions for Masonic labourers and employers. According to the meaning of the word *Three*, the apprentice has to prepare himself by extraction, and to pass from this to liberation, the freeing from the bond ; the craftsman has to look for guidance to the 5, i.e. Comprehension ; and the Master or employer, the self-made man, to the 7, i.e. Consummation or Return.*

When the various stages of the great becoming of the Cosmos, symbolized by the numbers one to seven, have been consummated, the broadening-out process commences ; for this consummation of the seven is not a completion, but a definite and final preparation to effect the completion symbolized by ten.

* The higher meaning is still deeper, and refers to Cosmic Energy and its "3, 5 and 7 Strides" in *The Secret Doctrine*.

CHAPTER XI

In Hebrew the word "eight" is written ShMNH. This, as will be seen, has a dual root, ShM and MUN, the former referring to the act of placing one thing upon another (D'Olivet), or of joining or placing a thing (Parkhurst), and the latter to distinguish by shape (D'Olivet). If spelt without the omissible U, the meaning is singularly appropriate, viz. to distribute by number, or by parts, the evolving of different groupings of the atoms which go to form the natural elements.

The first seven figure-symbols represent, as has been seen, the preparation and completion of the Cosmic Field. Through these processes, the once formless Matter has become polarized, affinitized, stabilized, and atomized, stamped with the hallmark of different rhythms. Now comes eight, the symbol of the differentiation of definite forms, and the reflection or double of four, the symbol of foundation, the "squaring-up" process.

Here the Hermetic axiom "as above so below" is singularly appropriate. This is shown clearly in the Hebrew word, the letter N, joined to the symbols of duration (Sh), plasticity (M), and life (H), referring to the process of individualization, the development of definiteness, which is the special work of the epoch symbolized by the number eight.

ShMNH thus gives the key to the fundamental

meaning of the ideas expressed in this number—
the heaping of atom upon atom, of molecule upon
molecule, and the aggregation of forms resulting
from this growth of elements and its development.

Now, whereas the number four represents the
foundation of all things in an original Root-Substance, spread out, as it were, in readiness for creation, the number eight, its double, represents a
completed foundation in actually atomized and,
therefore, manifested matter.

Numerical stages are thus repeated, and geometry
rather than arithmetic becomes the law. The atoms,
as points, range themselves as lines, and these lines
form up into triangles which, in order to produce
solids, must reflect themselves as fours, because four
is the number of foundation and therefore the first
plan of a solid figure. In this way the atoms formed
into triangles reflect themselves to produce "foured"
triangles, arranged upon a triangular base, and
thus give rise to what is called the tetrahedron, a
four-sided and solidly triangular figure. Other shapes
are formed in the same manner, as may be proved by
a study of the internal arrangement of the different
atoms forming the base of the various elements.*

The manifestation of solid and enclosing bodies
necessitates what may be termed crystallization, and
this produces many different modifications. It is, of
course, obvious that no actual building of forms is possible in a universe unless the plastic Substance is separated into definite and individual parts. These parts,
atoms, or electrons, circular forms with central "points"
within them, show again that point-in-the-circle idea

---

* See especially *Occult Chemistry,* by Annie Besant and C. W·
Leadbeater.

which is the true symbol of Nature. Without this atomization, as already seen, all would remain a flux of undifferentiated Substance ; moreover, the atoms themselves, left to exercise their independence, could never build a universe. Held together, however, by the affinitizing Power within, atom revolves intriguingly around atom, and groups of atoms are thus synthesized and welded into different geometrical forms, and solid or enclosing figures produced.

Thus the meaning inherent in the Hebrew word for eight expresses, as a word, the innermost idea of the eight process.

It should again be noted that there are three preparations for the formation of solid matter : the first, as symbolized by the number two, is the stage in which Root-Substance is polarized from the One-ness which contains in Itself Life and Substance, not as separate and definite opposites, but as an undifferentiated Reality. The second preparation is the quaternizing process during which this polarized Substance (Two) is prepared as a foundation for the many degrees of matter eventually produced from it. The final preparation is in the eight stage, where matter is heaped upon matter, and the "elements" are definitely built up. These preparations may be symbolized in arithmetic as 2^3, the cube root of 8, the third power of 2, $2 \times 2 \times 2 = 8$.

After the atomization of matter, the "sevening" process, all is ready for the building-up of material forms, and atom is linked to atom to produce molecules, which are in turn aggregated as elements. It should be noted that the "atom" of modern science is now seen to be an enclosed space in which electrons, or smaller atoms, revolve round a central nucleus ; it is, in fact, a solar system in miniature. The actual atom is, however, the primordial atom, not the atom of the scientists, which is, as they are discovering, really a collection of atoms.

The power of the number eight was held by the Greeks to be so great that a proverb was founded upon it : "All things are eight."* It is also curious to note, since the number is associated with the elementalization of matter, that the late Sir William Crookes, in his lecture to the Royal Society,† arranged the elements discovered in lines of "figures of eight", an arrangement which has since been found to be practically correct.‡

The Pythagoreans bestowed many queer names on this number, not all of which, however, have been understood. It was called *Universal Harmony, Mother* and *Rhea, Love* and *Friendship, Conception, Law, Immature* and *Justice.* The use of these names in this connection is to be understood, in some ways, according to the arithmetical power of the number, and in others as relating to the creation of the Universe ; it is, however, the latter only with which we are here concerned.

Thus the idea of Universal Harmony applied to the number eight is not difficult to understand when we remember the grouping of the atoms to produce the so-called Platonic Solids, and the grouping of these to the molecules which are the base of all elements, and which, in their turn, produce the many different grades of matter, visible and invisible. In the same way, the word *Mother* is a correct

* *Theoretic Arithmetic*, Thomas Taylor, p. 212.
† *Proceedings*, June 9th, 1898.
‡ See *Occult Chemistry*, p. 12, first edition.

description, and with the word *Rhea* (Mother Nature) expresses the idea that all forms proceed from the process symbolized by this number. *Love* and *Friendship, Conception, Law* and *Justice*, are, likewise, all clearly understandable in this connection, and the idea that the number represented that which was *immature* is especially helpful, inasmuch as the process of aggregation is alone the real beginning of bodies.

It is interesting to note, in passing, that some writers consider that eight represents that Law of Cause and Effect which is called *Karma* by the Hindus, *Kismet* by the Mohammedans, and *Judgments* by the Hebrews.

The mode of the creation of geometrical forms is difficult of understanding without the definite and rational use of the imagination, the image-forming faculty of the mind. Thus, let it be imagined that a certain point ("that which has position but no magnitude") in Space be viewed as from above. The point, having to produce a form, goes off "downwards "in three lines, at right angles to each other, and these are founded in the matter below on a triangular base, thus forming the Tetrahedron, i.e. four equilateral triangles.

Now, whereas four represents a "superficial" foundation, eight symbolizes a solid foundation, and hence was called the "First Cube" by the Pythagoreans. In other words, eight is the Crystallization which is prior to Materialization. The whole process may be summed up as *aggregation*, or *Intassement des formes*, to quote an expression of D'Olivet's. Moreover, even the shape of the letter, as originally written, was itself two squares, one posed upon the other, §. This became the modern 8, the only completely closed figure.

CHAPTER XII

As the number six symbolizes the balancing-up of the Spirit-Matter "opposites" of the Universe for creative purposes, so, this work completed, atoms, positive and negative, "male" and "female", are formed by the "seven-ing" process, and are then drawn together, by affinity of origin, and revolve around each other, forming a relatively stable duality. Seven being thus the completion of the preparatory stages of creation, numbering commences anew.

The next phase, that of formation, or *intassement des formes*, is symbolized by the number eight. In this, the atoms, coming together, serve as a basis for the different elements, matter being heaped upon matter, atom on atom, and the consequent aggregations crystallized into geometrical forms which take shape according to the atomic combination underlying them, as has been shown.

The number nine represents a new stage in the development, i.e. the differentiation of elements into compounds, resulting in seven kinds of matter, ranging from the finest to the densest. Hence the number nine is here accepted as representing change, a trinitized trinity.

The *Ennead*, or nine, "was celebrated by the Pythagoreans as flowing round the other numbers within the decad, or ten, like the ocean". This strange and mystical allusion would seem to refer to the fact that the stage of creation represented by the number nine is that in which all forms were made ready to be built up into bodies, and included in themselves all shapes, and hence all numbers, geometrically considered. Thus the stage comprehended all numbers within itself, and so was correctly described as "flowing round" them.

Nine was also called the *horizon*, probably because it is the approach towards the completion symbolized by ten, and hence signified that which was farthest away from the beginning. This idea is explained arithmetically by the anonymous writer quoted by Taylor :

That there can be no number beyond the ennead, but that it circulates all numbers within itself, is evident from the regression of numbers. For the natural progression of them is as far as nine, but after it their retrogression takes place. For 10 becomes, as it were, again the Monad (the One). Thus if from each of the numbers 10, 11, 12, 13, 14, 15, 16, 17, 18, and 19 the number 9 is subtracted, the numbers that remain will be 1, 2, 3, 4, 5, 6, 7, 8, 9, 10, and *vice versa* the progression will receive an increase by the addition of nine. For if to each of the numbers 1, 2, 3, 4, 5, etc., 9 is added, the numbers produced will be 10, 11, 12, 13, 14, etc. Likewise by subtracting from 20 twice 9, from 30 thrice 9, from 40 four times 9, from 50 five times 9, etc., the numbers 2, 3, 4, 5, 6, etc., will be produced. By taking likewise from 100 11 times 9 we again return to the Monad, and after the same manner we may proceed to infinity. Hence it is not possible there should be any elementary number beyond the ennead (nine). Hence they called it Ocean and Horizon, because all numbers are comprehended by and revolve within it.*

* *Theoretic Arithmetic,* p. 205.

Since this number represents, as a cosmic process, a distinct change of condition, a *turning* from the formless to a bodily creation, it is well named *Terpsichore*, although it may also be understood arithmetically, as Taylor says, quoting his anonymous author once more. In this sense, nine was called *Terpsichore*, the Dancing Muse, "because of its turning and causing the retrogression and convergency of productive principles to circulate like a dance".

Nine thus represents the stage wherein a distinct change is made, and this is seen cosmically in the perfect balance of all things, three trinities in one. It represents the perfect balancing of all produced and atomized matter. Matter, qualified under number five and atomized under seven, has now to be arranged into states. As, however, all manifestation is triune, whether Matter or Spirit, and as one manifesting as trinity becomes seven, so there are now seven main gradations of matter, each atomized. From these all bodies are produced.

These seven are fundamental divisions of matter, but each of them has, in turn, by combination and grading, seven sub-divisions. These seven appear everywhere in a completely manifested universe. Hence in the process symbolized by the number nine, seven is a subsidiary arrangement.*

In Hebrew, nine is called TShO. This word contains the sign of relative duration (Sh) added to the sign of materiality (O), and governed by the

---

* The Koran states that God created 7 Heavens and 7 Earths (lxvi2; xli8-11). Sufis speaks of seven planes in Nature, as do Hindus and Theosophists generally. Islam has its seven inferior worlds, and Judaism its seven Heavens.

K

Tauf or Tau, which represents reciprocity, perfection, and the all-embracing Universal Soul. It is, therefore, a sign that the work of creation is nearing its completion, and that a change is due. This idea is mentioned also by H. P. Blavatsky, who says :

> The Egyptian Cross, or Tau, is the Alpha and Omega of the Secret Doctrine Wisdom, which is symbolized by the initial and final letters of Thot (Hermes). Thot was the inventor of the Egyptian alphabet, and the letter Tau closed the alphabets of the Jews and the Samaritans, *who called this* character the "end" or "perfection", "culmination" and "security".*

It is clear from these symbols that nine represents the final stage of preparation or "creation", in which all things are formed, shaped up, and materialized ready for the change which leads to completion.

Nine, as we have seen, is a reflection of the Three on the lowest planes, as six is its reflection in the intermediate world. Each of these trinities—3, 6, and 9—represent the same work in different worlds. The first belongs to the world of Ideation, the Archetypal or *Atzilatic* World ; the second to the World of *Briah*, the Creative World ; and the last to the dense world of forms.† Their work, whether in the archetypal or lower worlds of dense matter, is the same, viz. the connecting and relating of the "opposites" by means of Cosmic Energy, the "Base" or Connecting Link. Hence the symbol 9 represents, in this respect, the final inter-relating in

---

* *The Secret Doctrine*, vol. ii, p. 614.
† The 12 may be referred to the purely physical and lower worlds, the *Asiah*.

the world of forms and the ensuing relationships of Knower, Known, and Knowledge, of Self, Not-Self, and the Relation between them.

D'Olivet says of this number :

The root ShO (עש), which signifies ordinarily *chalk*, *cement*, carries with it all ideas of cementing, of consolidation, restoration, preservation, etc. The verb עוש (ShUO), which is derived from it, expresses the action of cementing, coating, or carefully closing. Therefore the name of the number in question being clearly composed of this root, עש (ShO), governed by the sign of reciprocity, ought to be understood as a cementing or mutual consolidation. It bears a very intimate relation with the number three, of which it is a power, comprising likewise the ideas of preservation and salvation.

CHAPTER XIII

THE Decad, ten, was called many strange names by the Pythagoreans, such as *the world, heaven unwearied, fate, eternity, Atlas, strength, necessity*. It was named *Decad* because it contains all things in itself, and *the world* because all things are arranged according to it, both partially and universally. It was also *the universal recipient, the boundary of all things*, and *unwearied*.* Hence it was called *eternity*, because it contains all things in itself, and probably for the same reason was named *Atlas*, he who, according to the Greek myth, bears the whole world on his shoulders. It was called strength because it was the completion of all things, matter expanded into physicality, hence solid and strong.

Ten denotes the completion of building, whether the body of man or the universe, and the emanation of the Beings who ensoul such bodies. It is thus the number of a complete but complex unity, a being or thing, a body which is unique and yet contains in itself innumerable parts, each of which, although belonging to the common unity, is also complete in itself. It is thus the completed Process. After it, the same series is repeated, but the fundamental idea is ever the same.

The complete unfolding of creation is clearly a

---

* *Theoretic Arithmetic*, Taylor, p. 208.

series of progressions, or numbers, ending in ten, which is a new kind of collective unity, different from the one which begins all things, inasmuch as it is One fully developed as a unified collectivity, a many-ness, and yet a oneness. Hence, although the stage of ten represents completion it is itself an effect, and, as such, a new generating cause, as may be easily understood by considering man as a symbol of this process, for man is the result of such a series, as a study of embryology and biology will show. He is a result, a ten, and as such he becomes a cause, as parent of similar numberings, or genetic progressions. In this way, Man, the smaller world, may justly be compared with the Universe, the greater world.

Ten therefore represents the stage when all is complete. It shows the formation of bodies and actual forms, whether of man or of the worlds in Space. It is, in a sense, an end of creation, yet as there is no absolute end and no absolute beginning in That which is Illimitable, it is at once an end and a beginning, an effect and the new cause which arises therefrom.

Hence ten cannot be called the "complete number" in the sense of an absolute end. Rather is it the Perfect Number. Dr. Allendy calls it the collective being, unity realized, and the universe itself. These descriptions exactly coincide with what has been stated herein. He confirms also what has been said regarding the two kinds of Unity expressed in the one and the ten :

"It is well", he says, "to make a distinction between the synthetic unity expressed by the number one and the composite ten. Both may serve to designate composites in any particular individuality ; the organic molecule formed of atoms, the living cell formed from molecules, the organism itself formed from cells, etc. Each of these unities is a relative unity or singularity, comprehending only a part of the sub-unities which exist in the world, and which are themselves found to be comprised in a whole of a still superior order ; but the difference between them corresponds to the fact that simple unity is an odd number and the unity of the ten an even number."

It should, however, be noted that although seven is the full extent of Unity unfolded, it is not generative, as is the complete ten. This is made very clear in Fabre D'Olivet's table, as will be seen.

Ten is the symbol of completion, the completion of a whole process, and therefore distinct from the completion of a part, which is the result of the "seven-ing" process, or consummation, and is represented by the number 7. Man, the microcosm, is sevenfold, and his work is to synthesize his seven "principles" and know himself as one. This is "peace and consummation sweet" ; but until he has also realized the Monad and its triple powers, he cannot complete the cycle and become the ten. Thus the Perfect Man is the Seven, and the God-man the ten. There may be a final step in the direction of the 12, which is the four-fold completion, but of this we have no adequate knowledge.

The interested reader is referred to the description of the different numbers given in *The Secret Doctrine*. The meanings given them herein have been evolved upon other lines, complementary, it is true, though to the superficial eye totally unrelated. But it is well to remember that *The Secret Doctrine* is *the* book of all modern "occult" books, and its *dicta* the *dicta* of a master in the Science of Numbers. Dealing with the word ten, H. P. Blavatsky says :

Ten, or the Decad, brings all these digits back to unity, and ends the Pythagorean table. Hence this figure—unity within zero—was the symbol of Deity, of the Universe, and of Man. Such is the secret meaning of "the strong grip of the lion's paw, of the tribe of Judah" (the master-mason's grip) between two hands, the joint number of whose fingers is *ten.*

This Decad, representing the Universe and its evolution out of Silence and the unknown depths of the Spiritual Soul or Anima Mundi, presented two sides or aspects to the student. It could be, and was at first, applied to the Macrocosm, after which it descended to the Microcosm, or man. There was, then, the purely materialistic or "surface science", both of which could be expounded by and contained in the Decad. It could be studied, in short, both by the deductive method of Plato, and the inductive method of Aristotle. The former started from a divine comprehension, when the plurality proceeded from unity, or the digits of the Decad appeared, only to be finally reabsorbed, lost in the infinite Circle. The latter depended on sensuous perception, when the Decad could be regarded either as the unity that multiplies, or matter which differentiates ; its study being limited to the plane surface, to the cross, or the *seven* which proceed from the *ten*, or the perfect number, on Earth as in Heaven.*

"Only with the eyes closed", i.e. by deep meditation, said the ancient Qabalists, "can Three be

---

* *The Secret Doctrine*, vol. ii, pp. 614 and 605.

seen as One," and only in the same way can the inner meaning of the Ten be fully comprehended. Yet it is possible to give some explanation of the mystery by means of the letters OSR (עשׂר) which form the word. The governing sign, O, is a symbol of materiality or aggregation, the former being its meaning on the lower planes, and the latter on the higher; the S is the sign of relative duration and movement, and the R of *progress*, of the fire which tends ever upwards, and of the *renewal* of things. Hence it is not difficult to realize that *Ten* is the symbol of *Completion*, whether the preparatory completion before the beginning (as in the fœtus), or the completion after a "beginning" or birth. The symbols of *aggregation*, *relative duration*, *progress*, and *renewal* are therefore rightly used to form the word *Ten*.

It should be remembered and clearly understood that a completion must come before the birth or beginning, as well as after it, whether on the physical or on formless levels. In the cosmic "birth", we find that until the Ten Sephiroth, the Ten *Prajapati*, are emanated, no "creation" is possible, and likewise, before the nine months have passed, the child is not born as a complete individual. This shows also that each completed revolution, each *Ten*, has within it the potency of a new round of manifestation.

It is interesting to note that one of the root meanings of this word, viz. SR, or Seer, means *to govern*, *to direct*, *to rule*, hence our word Seer in the sense of *Prophet*. More wonderful still is its other meaning, especially when it is remembered that one completion has in it *that which is attached to* the seed of a

new revolution. This meaning, "umbilical cord", *
gives a deep hint as to the relation of the fœtus and
its development to the birth and development of the
Cosmos.

D'Olivet tells us that the word OSR refers to the
collecting together of power, of the elementary
motive force. Its root, OS, refers to aggregation,
and from it we get the verb OSUH, *to do, to make.*
The second root, SR, is the moving principle of
anything, and it gives us the verb SUR, meaning
to direct, to govern. Ten is, according to this authority,
aggregation and *reformative power.*

There is certainly some strong connection between
this Hebrew word for ten (OSR) and the Egyptian
Osiris, which is spelt in various ways : *User, Oser,
As-ar,* and *Usr-Rā.* The last has nearly the same
letters as the Hebrew, with the addition of the vowel,
which is an interpolation. Osiris, or *Usra,* was the
Egyptian "god of the dead", and ten, it will be
remembered, is the symbol of death and resurrection, i.e. birth into other conditions. In later times,
according to Wallis Budge,† *Osiris* was called
Unnefer, which means "he who makes manifest the
good", and is the sign of the regenerator. This
is seen from a verse in the *Book of the Dead,* where
certain words are put into the mouth of the God :
"I am Yesterday, and I am To-day ; and I have the
power to be born a second time. I, the hidden soul,
create the gods, and I give sepulchral meals to the
divine beings in Amenti and in heaven."‡

The idea of destruction and regeneration is also seen
in the legend of Osiris and Typhon. Typhon finds

---

* Ezek. xvi, 4.   Prov. iii, 8.
† *Gods of the Egyptians,* vol. ii, p. 114.   ‡ *Ibid.,* p. 116.

the body of Osiris, which has been hidden by Isis, and he dismembers it and *scatters the fragments*; but "his limbs had been reconstructed and he had become immortal . . . his body never decayed like the bodies of ordinary men",* and *it never diminished, even in death.* Here is a deep teaching for those who know the Secret Doctrine !

It is easy to realize that the Hebrews spoiled the Egyptians of much that was of value, since here is a most precious jewel, the ten, OSR, taken from the name Osiris, symbol of death, of resurrection, and of completion, the perfection of man.

This mystery of creation and completion symbolized by the number ten is also told in guarded language in the tenth chapter of the Book of Genesis, a chapter which contains secrets and mysteries said to be confided in fullness only during Initiation. The verses relating to the progeny of Noah (here symbolizing the *Manu* or God) tell of the functions of the different Orders of Beings, and their Armies of Helpers, the Cosmic Hierarchy, whose appearance and make-up is explained in such a manner as to be ever hidden from all save those who have the key.

The letter Yod, which in Hebrew stands for ten, well represents, as a figure, the Primordial Point which contains all things *in potentia.* It is the sign of manifestation *par excellence*, and means, literally, *hand* or *pointing finger.* All the Hebrew letters are made from it and all things emanate from it, for as ten, or Completion, it contains all numbers in itself ($1 + 2 + 3 + 4 = 10$). It is the *Lingam* (1) and *Yoni* (0) combined, the Divine Hermaphrodite,

---

* *Ibid.*, vol. ii, p. 140.

the actual point from which all flows, even on the physical plane. It is also a *picture* of the sperm-cell which fertilizes the ovum. This shows that in the Yod is contained the Secret of Evolution and the Purpose of Life.

Fabre D'Olivet says :

The number *ten* has this peculiarity in the language of numbers, that *it is at once final and initial*; that is to say *it terminates the first decade and commences the second*, thus enclosing two expressions, and presenting itself at the same time as term and principle. I beg the reader to examine the following example of a thing which is difficult to understand otherwise.

FIRST DECADE	SECOND DECADE	THIRD DECADE
1 2 3 4 5 6 7 8 9 10 11	12 13 14 15 16 17 18 19 20 21	22 23 24 25 etc.
1 2 3 4 5 6 7 8	9 10 11 12 13 14 15 16 etc.
1 2 3 4 5 6 7 etc.

We see in this example that the number ten of the first decade corresponds to the number 1 of the second ; in such wise that if we follow the arithmetical progression from one to another we find that the corresponding numbers are 10 and 1, 11 and 2, 12 and 3, etc., always adding the members of the complex numbers in order to form a simple number.

Now I ought to say for those of my readers who do not fear new or profound ideas that the first ten chapters of Genesis do not correspond to the first decade as explained above, but to the second : it is as if the idea were that this book had a beginning composed of nine chapters of which the first of Genesis formed the tenth. This commencement was consecrated to Theogony, and turned upon the essence of Divinity. I have strong reasons for thinking that Moses, having received from the sanctuary of Thebes these theogonic principles, suppressed them, not thinking, with good reason, that the Hebrews were in any way able to comprehend them.*

That this number Ten represents Completion and Perfection is also shown by the fact that it is the complete and final number, all others being evolved from it, or from its components. All numbers are built up from the primordial one, two, and three, and the first step from this trinity, the junction of one and three, gives four, and from these all numbers originate, their total being ten. Without a manifested trinity of number nothing can be produced, for $1+2=3$, $3+1=4$, $3+2=5$, $3+2+1=6$, $4+3=7$, $4+3+1=8$, $3+2+4=9$, $1+2+3+4=10$. Beyond this all is repetition and multiplication. Hence 10 is rightly named the Perfect Number, for all numbers subsist therein.

Ten is thus the symbol of Completion and of a new beginning, of coming and going, of *Pralaya* and *Manvantara*, of Rest and Activity, and, as such, is a fitting symbol wherewith to end this work. For it is itself in the nature of a *Ten*, complete in itself, yet unending, since it contains within it the seeds of further *Tens* which abler students may bring to completion. If it has that result, it will have served its purpose.

---

* *La Langue Hébraique Restituée*, vol. ii.

FINIS

Ibis Press
Western Mystery Tradition Series

Available at your local bookstore or by ordering direct from our distributor, Red Wheel/Weiser, P.O. Box 612, York Beach, ME, 03910; Phone: 1-800-423-7087; Fax: 1-877-337-3309; orders@redwheelweiser.com

The Adornment of the Spiritual Marriage with The Book of Truth & The Sparkling Stone

Jan van Rusbroeck.
Translated by C. A. Wynschenk Dom.
New Introduction by
Allan Armstrong.
A classic for students of Christian mysticism.
$16.95 • Paper
288 pages • 5 ½ x 8 ½
ISBN 0-89254-140-7

The Book of Jubilees or The Little Genesis

Translated by
Robert Henry Charles.
New Foreword by
R. A. Gilbert.
Apocryphal text detailing events from the Creation to the life of Moses.
$14.95 • Paper
232 pages • 5 ½ x 8 ½
ISBN 0-89254-137-7

The Book of Formation, or Sepher Yetzirah

Attributed to
Rabbi Akiba ben Joseph.
Translated by Knut Stenring.
Introduced and
edited by A. E. Waite.
New Foreword by R. A. Gilbert.
*Contains a unique "Master Key to the
Theoretical and Practical Kabala,"
and an ingenious article by
H. S. Redgrove, "The Mathematics
of the* Sepher Yetzirah."
$14.95 • Paper
96 pages • 6 x 9 •
Line art and foldout
ISBN: 0-89254-094-X

Dionysius the Areopagite on the Divine Names and the Mystical Theology

Translated by C. E. Rolt.
New Preface by
Alan Armstrong.
*A clear and insightful
translation of two important works of
Neo-Platonic Christian mysticism.*
$16.95 • Paper
240 pages • 5 ½ x 8 ½
ISBN: 0-89254-095-8

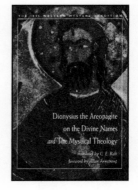

The House of the Hidden Places
and
The Book of the Master

W. Marsham Adams.
New Foreword by R. A. Gilbert.
Explore the hidden meaning of the
Great Pyramid of Giza and the
Egyptian Ritual of the Dead.
$24.95 • Paper
512 pages • 5 ½ x 8 ½
Illustrations and one foldout
ISBN: 0-89254-092-3

John Dee
Charlotte Fell Smith.
New Foreword by R. A. Gilbert.
A collector's edition of the seminal,
no-nonsense biography of 14th-century
scientist and magician John Dee.
$55.00 • Hardcover
368 pages • 6 x 9
8 plates
ISBN 0-89254-104-0

Serpent Myths of Ancient Egypt

William Ricketts Cooper.
*Explores the serpent symbolism of
ancient Egypt and its role in
the Ritual of the Dead.*
$10.95 • Paper
96 pages • 5 ½ x 8 ½
127 Illustrations.
ISBN 0-89254-139-3

Theurgy, or the Hermetic Practice:
A Treatise on Spiritual Alchemy

E. J. Langford Garstin.
New Foreword by
Edward Dunning.
*A succinct guide to alchemical symbolism
and spiritual practice.*
$12.95 • Paper
160 pages • 5 ½ x 8 ½
ISBN: 0-89254-091-5